TestSMART

for
Math Concepts

Grade 3

Help for

Basic Math Skills

State Competency Tests

Achievement Tests

by

Lori Mammen

These popular teacher resources and activity books are available from ECS Learning Systems, Inc. for grades K–6.

Basic Skills Software for Math	Gr. 1-10	240 Lessons
Basic Skills Software for Reading	Gr. 1-10	405 Lessons
The Bright Blue Thinking Books™	Ages 6–12	3 Titles
Building Language Power	Gr. 4–9	3 Titles
Foundations for Writing	Gr. 2–8	2 Titles
Get Writing!!™	Gr. K–5	6 Titles
Graphic Organizer Collection	Gr. 3–12	1 Title
Home Study Collection™	Gr. 1–6	18 Titles
Inkblots™	Gr. K–6	2 Titles
The Little Red Writing Books™	Ages 6–12	3 Titles
Math Whiz Kids™	Gr. 3–5	4 Titles
Novel Extenders™	Gr. 1–6	7 Titles
On the Chalkboard™	Gr. 1–6	6 Titles
Once Upon a Time™ for Emerging Readers	Gr. K–2	10 Titles
Once Upon a Time™ (Books + Tapes)	Gr. K–2	10 Titles
The Picture Book Companion	Gr. K–3	3 Titles
Quick Thinking™	Gr. K–6	1 Title
Springboards for Reading	Gr. 3–6	2 Titles
Structures for Reading, Writing, Thinking	Gr. 4–9	4 Titles
Test Preparation Guides	Gr. 2–12	41 Titles
Wake Up, Brain!!™	Gr. 1–6	6 Titles
Writing Warm-Ups™	Gr. K–6	2 Titles

To order, or for a complete catalog, write:

ECS Learning Systems, Inc.
P.O. Box 791439
San Antonio, Texas 78279-1439
Web site: www.educyberstor.com

or contact your local school supply store.

Cover: Kirstin Simpson
Book Design: Educational Media Services

ISBN 1–57022–240-1

Printed in the United States of America.

Contents

Welcome to *TestSMART* ™!!

It's just the tool you need
to help students review important mathematics skills and
prepare for standardized mathematics tests!

Introduction

During the past several years, an increasing number of American students have faced some form of state-mandated competency testing in mathematics. While several states use established achievement tests, such as the Iowa Test of Basic Skills (ITBS), to assess students' achievement in mathematics, other states' assessments focus on the skills and knowledge emphasized in their particular mathematics curriculum. Texas, for example, has administered the state-developed Texas Assessment of Academic Skills (TAAS) since 1990. The New York State Testing Program began in 1999 and tests both fourth- and eighth-grade students in mathematics.

Whatever the testing route, one point is very clear: the trend toward more and more competency testing is widespread and intense. By the spring of 1999, 48 states had adopted some type of assessment for students at various grade levels. In some states, these tests are "high-stakes" events that determine whether a student is promoted to the next grade level in school.

The emphasis on competency tests has grown directly from the national push for higher educational standards and accountability. Under increasing pressure from political leaders, business people, and the general public, policy-makers have turned to testing as a primary way to measure and improve student performance. Although experienced educators know that such test results can reveal only a small part of a much broader educational picture, state-mandated competency tests have gained a strong foothold. Teachers must find effective ways to help their students prepare for these tests—and this is where *TestSMART* ™ plays an important role.

What's inside this book?

Designed to help students review and practice important reading and test-taking skills, *TestSMART* ™ includes reproducible practice exercises in the following areas—

- pretests for each of the five major objectives addressed in the book
- practice exercises that target the specific skills tested within each objective

In addition, each *TestSMART* ™ book includes—

- a master skills list based on mathematics standards of several states
- complete answer keys

The content of *TestSMART* ™ is outlined below.

Major Objectives: This book focuses on five major mathematics objectives which represent broad areas of understanding generally common to all grade levels. These objectives focus on developing students' understanding of—

- number concepts
- mathematical relations, functions, and other algebraic concepts
- geometric properties and relationships
- measurement concepts using metric and customary units
- probability and statistics

Specific Skills: A list of specific skills appears below each major objective. These skills represent appropriate grade-level expectations for a given objective.

Pretests: Five pretests are included in this book. Each pretest addresses one of the major objectives and includes test items for all the specific skills included with that objective. Teachers use the pretests to diagnose the students' areas of strength and weakness for a given objective.

Practice Exercises: Practice exercises follow each pretest. Unlike the pretests, each practice exercise addresses a specific skill. Teachers use the practice exercises to target specific areas of weakness revealed in the pretests.

Master Skills List/Correlation Chart: The mathematics skills addressed in *TestSMART* ™ are based on the mathematics standards and/or test specifications from several different states. No two states have identical wordings for their skills lists, but there are strong similarities from one state's list to another. The Master Skills List for Mathematics (page 7) represents a synthesis of the mathematics skills emphasized in various states. Teachers who use this book will recognize the skills that are stressed, even though the wording of a few objectives may vary slightly from that found in their own state's test specifications.

The Master Skills Correlation Chart (page 8) offers a place to identify the skills common to both *TestSMART* ™ and a specific state competency test. To show how such a correlation can be done, the author has included a sample correlation which shows the skills addressed in both *TestSMART* ™ and the skills tested on the Texas Assessment of Academic Skills (TAAS).

Answer Keys: Complete answer keys appear on pages 121–124.

How to Use This Book

Effective Test Preparation: What is the most effective way to prepare students for any mathematics competency test? Experienced educators know that the best test preparation includes three critical components—

- a strong curriculum that includes the content and skills to be tested
- effective and varied instructional methods that allow students to learn content and skills in many different ways
- targeted practice that familiarizes students with the specific content and format of the test they will take

Obviously, a strong curriculum and effective, varied instructional methods provide the foundation for all appropriate test preparation. Contrary to what some might believe, merely "teaching the test" performs a great disservice to students. Students must acquire knowledge, practice skills, and have specific educational experiences which can never be included on tests limited by time and in scope. For this reason, books like *TestSMART*™ should **never** become the heart of the curriculum or a replacement for strong instructional methods.

Targeted Practice: *TestSMART*™ does, however, address the final element of effective test preparation (targeted test practice) in the following ways—

- *TestSMART*™ familiarizes students with the content usually included in competency tests
- *TestSMART*™ familiarizes students with the general format of such tests

When students become familiar with both the content and the format of a test, they know what to expect on the actual test. This, in turn, improves their chances for success.

Using *TestSMART*™: Used as part of the regular curriculum, *TestSMART*™ allows teachers to—

- pretest skills needed for the actual test students will take
- determine students' areas of strength and/or weakness
- provide meaningful test-taking practice for students
- ease students' test anxiety
- communicate test expectations and content to parents

Master Skills List

I. Demonstrate an understanding of number concepts

A. Use place value to recognize, read, write (symbols and words), and describe the value of whole numbers
B. Use place value to compare and order whole numbers
C. Round numbers to the nearest ten, hundred, and thousand
D. Use fraction names and symbols to describe and compare fractional parts of whole objects or sets of objects
E. Determine the value of a collection of coins and bills
F. Read, write, compare, and order decimals expressed to hundredths

II. Demonstrate an understanding of mathematical relations, functions, and other algebraic concepts

A. Identify and extend whole-number and geometric patterns to make predictions and solve problems
B. Identify patterns in number sentences (fact families)
C. Solve problems involving numeric equations or inequalities
D. Identify patterns in a table of related number pairs based on a real-life situation and generate or extend the table

III. Demonstrate an understanding of geometric properties and relationships

A. Name, describe, and compare shapes and solids, using formal geometric vocabulary
B. Identify congruent shapes
C. Identify lines of symmetry in shapes
D. Locate and name points on a number line, using whole numbers and simple fractions

IV. Demonstrate an understanding of measurement concepts, using metric and customary units

A. Estimate, measure, and compare lengths using standard, customary, and metric units
B. Use linear measure to find the perimeter of a shape
C. Select appropriate units for a given measurement task
D. Carry out simple unit conversions within a system of measurement
E. Estimate the area of a figure by counting squares
F. Tell and write time shown on traditional and digital clocks
G. Identify or calculate elapsed time
H. Use a thermometer to measure temperature

V. Demonstrate an understanding of probability and statistics

A. Make predictions based on a sampling
B. Interpret information from pictographs, bar graphs, tables, and charts

Master Skills Correlation Chart

Use this chart to identify the *TestSMART* ™ skills included on a specific state competency test. To correlate the *TestSMART* ™ skills to a specific state's objectives, find and mark those skills common to both. The first column shows a sample correlation based on the Texas Assessment of Academic Skills (TAAS).

	Sample Correlation	
I. Demonstrate an understanding of number concepts		
A. Use place value to recognize, read, write (symbols and words), and describe the value of whole numbers	★	
B. Use place value to compare and order whole numbers	★	
C. Round numbers to the nearest ten, hundred, and thousand		
D. Use fraction names and symbols to describe and compare fractional parts of whole objects or sets of objects	★	
E. Determine the value of a collection of coins and bills	★	
F. Read, write, compare, and order decimals expressed to hundredths		
II. Demonstrate an understanding of mathematical relations, functions, and other algebraic concepts		
A. Identify and extend whole-number and geometric patterns to make predictions and solve problems	★	
B. Identify patterns in number sentences (fact families)	★	
C. Solve problems involving numeric equations or inequalities		
D. Identify patterns in a table of related number pairs based on a real-life situation and generate or extend the table	★	
III. Demonstrate an understanding of geometric properties/relationships		
A. Name, describe, and compare shapes and solids, using formal geometric vocabulary	★	
B. Identify congruent shapes	★	
C. Identify lines of symmetry in shapes	★	
D. Locate and name points on a number line, using whole numbers and simple fractions	★	
IV. Demonstrate an understanding of measurement concepts, using metric and customary units		
A. Estimate, measure, and compare lengths using standard, customary, and metric units	★	
B. Use linear measure to find the perimeter of a shape	★	
C. Select appropriate units for a given measurement task		
D. Carry out simple unit conversions within a system of measurement		
E. Estimate the area of a figure by counting squares		
F. Tell and write time shown on traditional and digital clocks	★	
G. Identify or calculate elapsed time		
H. Use a thermometer to measure temperature	★	
V. Demonstrate an understanding of probability and statistics		
A. Make predictions based on a sampling		
B. Interpret information from pictographs, bar graphs, tables, and charts	★	

Number Concepts

I. Demonstrate an understanding of number concepts

A. Use place value to recognize, read, write (symbols and words), and describe the value of whole numbers
B. Use place value to compare and order whole numbers
C. Round numbers to the nearest ten, hundred, and thousand
D. Use fraction names and symbols to describe and compare fractional parts of whole objects or sets of objects
E. Determine the value of a collection of coins and bills
F. Read, write, compare, and order decimals expressed to hundredths

Notes

Objective 1: Pretest

I.A Use place value to recognize, read, write (symbols and words), and describe the value of whole numbers (1–12)

1. Find the numeral that means 6 hundreds, 6 tens, and 2 ones.

0 **A** 626

0 **B** 662

0 **C** 6,062

0 **D** 6,602

2. Jody drove 2,636 miles on her vacation. This number is read—

0 **A** two hundred six thirty-six

0 **B** twenty-six thousand, six hundred thirty-six

0 **C** twenty thousand, six hundred thirty-six

0 **D** two thousand, six hundred thirty-six

3. Which number is greater than 2,013 but less than 2,208?

0 **A** 2,100

0 **B** 2,000

0 **C** 2,210

0 **D** 2,001

4. Find the number that is the same as 400 + 30 + 4.

0 **A** 740

0 **B** 704

0 **C** 470

0 **D** 434

5. Which one shows 1,210 written in expanded form?

0 **A** 1000 + 200 + 10

0 **B** 1000 + 200 + 1

0 **C** 1000 + 20 + 1

0 **D** 100 + 20 + 1

6. Which numeral means 8 hundreds, 3 tens, and 9 ones?

0 **A** 389

0 **B** 398

0 **C** 839

0 **D** 893

7. Three thousand, four hundred five is written—

0 **A** 345

0 **B** 3,045

0 **C** 3,405

0 **D** 3,450

8. What is the value of 3 in the number 1,238?

0 **A** 3 thousands

0 **B** 3 hundreds

0 **C** 3 tens

0 **D** 3 ones

9. The number 5,098 is written—

0 **A** five thousand, nine hundred eighty

0 **B** five thousand, nine hundred eight

0 **C** five thousand, ninety-eight

0 **D** five hundred, ninety-eight

10. Which one shows 6,071?

0 **A** 600 + 70 + 1

0 **B** 600 + 70 + 10

0 **C** 6000 + 700 + 1

0 **D** 6000 + 70 + 1

11. Find the number that is the same as 500 + 40 + 3.

0 **A** 5,430

0 **B** 5,403

0 **C** 543

0 **D** 507

12. Which number is 1,000 greater than 4,312?

0 **A** 5,312

0 **B** 4,412

0 **C** 4,322

0 **D** 4,313

I.B *Use place value to compare and order whole numbers (13–17)*

13. Which group shows the numbers in order **from greatest to least**?

0 **A** 63 74 59

0 **B** 71 48 39

0 **C** 26 19 40

0 **D** 64 75 95

14. Find the number that is between 145 and 190.

145 ______ 190

0 **A** 139

0 **B** 144

0 **C** 153

0 **D** 192

15. The list shows the number of students that go to four different schools.

School	**Students**
Nash	902
Clark	817
Bowie	610
Davis	763

Which group shows the schools in order **from least** number of students **to greatest** number of students?

0 **A** Bowie, Davis, Clark, Nash

0 **B** Nash, Davis, Bowie, Clark

0 **C** Bowie, Clark, Davis, Nash

0 **D** Clark, Bowie, Nash, Davis

16. Find the number that is between 973 and 1,102.

973 ______ 1,102

0 **A** 873

0 **B** 1,138

0 **C** 1,046

0 **D** 1,200

17. Which group shows the numbers in order **from least to greatest**?

0 **A** 432 234 324 423

0 **B** 423 432 324 234

0 **C** 324 234 423 432

0 **D** 234 324 423 432

I.C Round numbers to the nearest ten, hundred, and thousand (18–22)

18. Carrie and her family drove 637 miles in one week. Rounded to the nearest ten miles, they drove—

0 **A** 600 miles

0 **B** 630 miles

0 **C** 640 miles

0 **D** 650 miles

19. The horses at Sunshine Stables ate 3,246 pounds of hay in one week. Rounded to the nearest hundred pounds, how much hay did the horses eat?

0 **A** 3,300 pounds

0 **B** 3,250 pounds

0 **C** 3,200 pounds

0 **D** 3,000 pounds

20. Mr. Lee has driven 48,138 miles in his car. How many miles is this when rounded to the nearest thousand miles?

0 **A** 50,000 miles

0 **B** 49,000 miles

0 **C** 48,000 miles

0 **D** 48,100 miles

21. The local bakery used 3,452 pounds of flour in one year. How much flour is this when rounded to the nearest hundred pounds?

0 **A** 3,400 pounds

0 **B** 3,450 pounds

0 **C** 3,500 pounds

0 **D** 4,000 pounds

22. The number of fans who went to the All-Star Basketball Game is 35,218. How many fans is this when rounded to the nearest thousand?

0 **A** 36,000

0 **B** 35,300

0 **C** 35,200

0 **D** 35,000

***I.D** Use fraction names and symbols to describe and compare fractional parts of whole objects or sets of objects (23–29)*

23. What fraction of the circles is shaded?

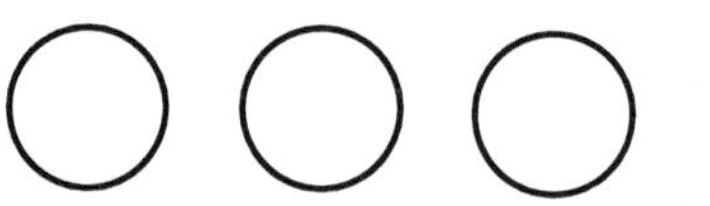

0 **A** $\frac{1}{2}$

0 **B** $\frac{1}{3}$

0 **C** $\frac{1}{4}$

0 **D** $\frac{3}{4}$

24. Which picture shows $\frac{1}{3}$ of the rectangle shaded?

0 **A** 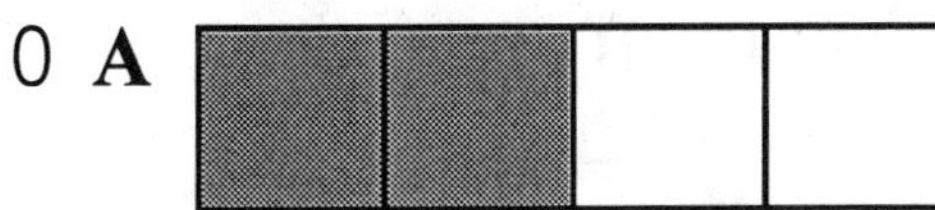

0 **B** 

0 **C** 

0 **D**

25. Which picture shows $\frac{1}{6}$ of the circles shaded?

0 **A** ●●○○○○

0 **B** ●●●○○○

0 **C** ○○●○○○

0 **D** ●●●●●○

26. Which set does NOT show $\frac{2}{4}$ of the circles shaded?

0 **A** ●●○○

0 **B** ●●●○

0 **C** ●○●○

0 **D** ○○●●

27. What fraction of the boxes is shaded?

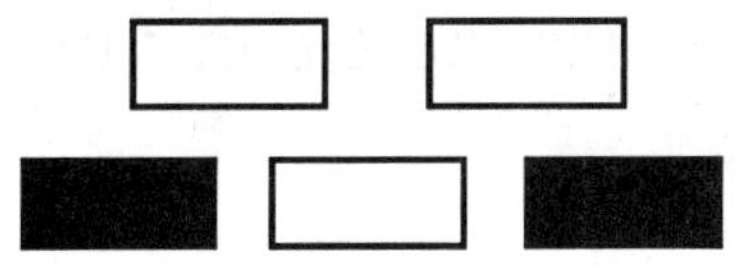

0 **A** $\frac{1}{5}$

0 **B** $\frac{2}{5}$

0 **C** $\frac{3}{5}$

0 **D** $\frac{4}{5}$

28. Which figure is NOT divided into halves?

0 **A**

0 **B**

0 **C**

0 **D**

29. Which fraction shows the greatest part of a whole?

0 **A** $\frac{1}{8}$

0 **B** $\frac{1}{6}$

0 **C** $\frac{1}{4}$

0 **D** $\frac{1}{2}$

I.E Determine the value of a collection of coins and bills (30–33)

30. Becky has these coins in her pocket.

How much money is this?

0 **A** 28¢

0 **B** 31¢

0 **C** 37¢

0 **D** 40¢

31. Nathan bought two candy bars. The clerk gave him these coins in change.

How much money is this?

0 **A** 63¢

0 **B** 58¢

0 **C** 43¢

0 **D** 33¢

32. How much money would you have if you had these coins and bills?

0 **A** $2.22

0 **B** $2.17

0 **C** $2.12

0 **D** $2.04

33. Cindy has these coins in her wallet.

How much money is this?

0 **A** 41¢

0 **B** 45¢

0 **C** 56¢

0 **D** 66¢

I.F Read, write, compare, and order decimals expressed to hundredths (34–39)

34. The runner won the race by two tenths of a second. How is this number written?

0 **A** 2.2

0 **B** 2.0

0 **C** 0.2

0 **D** 0.02

35. Which one shows the numbers in order **from least to greatest**?

0 **A** 1.12 1.22 1.2 1.02

0 **B** 1.02 1.12 1.2 1.22

0 **C** 1.22 1.2 1.12 1.02

0 **D** 1.2 1.22 1.12 1.02

36. Which number shows the **greatest** amount?

0 **A** 1.3

0 **B** 1.35

0 **C** 1.5

0 **D** 1.05

37. Which number tells how much is shaded?

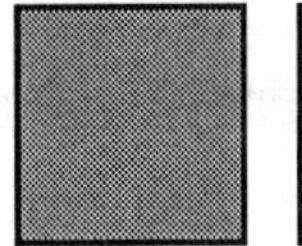 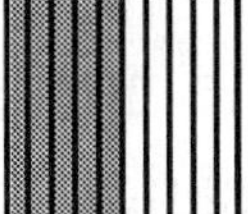

0 **A** 1.05

0 **B** 1.5

0 **C** 10.5

0 **D** 15

38. Which one shows the numbers in order **from greatest to least**?

0 **A** 1.19 1.09 0.19 1.9

0 **B** 1.19 1.9 1.09 0.19

0 **C** 1.9 1.19 1.09 0.19

0 **D** 0.19 1.09 1.19 1.9

39. How do you read the number 0.34?

0 **A** thirty-four

0 **B** three and four tenths

0 **C** thirty-four tenths

0 **D** thirty-four hundredths

Practice 1.A1

I.A Use place value to recognize, read, write (symbols and words), and describe the value of whole numbers

1. Find the numeral that means 7 thousands, 5 tens, and 3 ones.

0 **A** 7,530

0 **B** 7,503

0 **C** 7,053

0 **D** 753

2. Ken lives 2,035 miles from his cousin in Mexico. This number is read—

0 **A** two hundred, thirty-five

0 **B** twenty hundred, thirty-five

0 **C** two thousand, three hundred five

0 **D** two thousand, thirty-five

3. Which number is 100 more than 571?

0 **A** 671

0 **B** 561

0 **C** 570

0 **D** 471

4. Find the number that is the same as 6000 + 300 + 20 + 4.

0 **A** 9,024

0 **B** 6,306

0 **C** 6,324

0 **D** 924

5. Four thousand, two hundred fifteen is written—

0 **A** 42,015

0 **B** 40,215

0 **C** 4,251

0 **D** 4,215

6. What is the value of 9 in the number 40,923?

0 **A** 90 thousands

0 **B** 9 thousands

0 **C** 9 hundreds

0 **D** 9 tens

7. Which number is 1,000 less than 6,891?

0 **A** 7,891

0 **B** 6,881

0 **C** 6,791

0 **D** 5,891

Practice 1.A2

I.A Use place value to recognize, read, write (symbols and words), and describe the value of whole numbers

1. Find the numeral that means 8 thousands, 4 hundreds, 2 tens, and 3 ones.

0 **A** 12,023

0 **B** 8,423

0 **C** 8,342

0 **D** 8,243

2. The Goody-Goody Candy Store sells 2,150 pounds of candy every year. This number is read—

0 **A** twenty-one hundred five

0 **B** twenty thousand, one hundred fifty

0 **C** two thousand, fifteen

0 **D** two thousand, one hundred fifty

3. Which number is 2 hundreds less than 765?

0 **A** 565

0 **B** 745

0 **C** 763

0 **D** 965

4. Find the number that is the same as 7000 + 400 + 5.

0 **A** 745

0 **B** 7,405

0 **C** 7,450

0 **D** 70,450

5. Three hundred four is written–

0 **A** 3,400

0 **B** 340

0 **C** 314

0 **D** 304

6. What is the value of 4 in the number 40,923?

0 **A** 4 tens

0 **B** 4 hundreds

0 **C** 4 thousands

0 **D** 4 ten thousands

7. Which one shows 3,122?

0 **A** 31 + 20 + 2

0 **B** 300 + 100 + 20 + 2

0 **C** 3000 + 100 + 20 + 2

0 **D** 3000 + 100 + 2 + 2

Practice 1.A3

I.A Use place value to recognize, read, write (symbols and words), and describe the value of whole numbers

1. What is the value of 5 in the number 15,110?

0 **A** 5 tens

0 **B** 5 hundreds

0 **C** 5 thousands

0 **D** 5 ten thousands

2. Mrs. Banks wrote a check for $3,115. This number is read—

0 **A** thirty-one thousand, fifteen

0 **B** three thousand, one hundred fifteen

0 **C** three thousand, one hundred fifty-one

0 **D** three hundred fifteen

3. Which number is 4 tens more than 934?

0 **A** 4,934

0 **B** 1,334

0 **C** 974

0 **D** 938

4. Find the number that is the same as 5000 + 300 + 20 + 5.

0 **A** 53,205

0 **B** 5,505

0 **C** 5,325

0 **D** 825

5. Which one shows 9,046?

0 **A** 900 + 40 + 6

0 **B** 9000 + 400 + 60

0 **C** 9000 + 400 + 6

0 **D** 9000 + 40 + 6

6. Ten thousand, two hundred sixty-one is written—

0 **A** 12,601

0 **B** 12,062

0 **C** 10,261

0 **D** 1,261

7. What is the value of 3 in 9,039?

0 **A** 3 ones

0 **B** 3 tens

0 **C** 3 hundreds

0 **D** 3 thousands

Practice 1.B1

I.B Use place value to compare and order whole numbers

1. The list shows how much each of Tina's dogs weigh.

Dog	**Weight**
Rusty	64 pounds
Fluffy	57 pounds
Ernie	97 pounds
Bert	91 pounds

Which group shows the dogs in order **from heaviest to lightest**?

0 **A** Fluffy, Rusty, Bert, Ernie

0 **B** Ernie, Rusty, Bert, Fluffy

0 **C** Ernie, Bert, Rusty, Fluffy

0 **D** Rusty, Fluffy, Ernie, Bert

2. Find the number that is between 467 and 483.

467 ______ 483

0 **A** 492

0 **B** 453

0 **C** 429

0 **D** 472

3. Which group shows the numbers in order **from greatest to least**?

0 **A** 156 165 516 561

0 **B** 561 516 165 156

0 **C** 516 561 165 156

0 **D** 165 516 561 156

4. Which number shows the **greatest** amount?

0 **A** 1,019

0 **B** 1,109

0 **C** 1,901

0 **D** 1,190

5. Which number is greater than 532 but less than 613?

0 **A** 603

0 **B** 631

0 **C** 523

0 **D** 503

Practice 1.B2

1.B Use place value to compare and order whole numbers

1. The list shows the number of miles flown by four pilots.

Pilot	Miles
Robbins	3,271
Davis	3,095
Garza	3,309
Chang	3,401

Which pilot flew the **greatest** number of miles?

0 **A** Robbins

0 **B** Davis

0 **C** Garza

0 **D** Chang

2. Find the number that is between 1,112 and 1,259.

1,112 ______ 1,259

0 **A** 1,267

0 **B** 1,108

0 **C** 1,171

0 **D** 1,263

3. Which group shows the numbers in order **from least to greatest**?

0 **A** 561 529 643 650

0 **B** 529 643 650 561

0 **C** 650 643 561 529

0 **D** 529 561 643 650

4. Which number shows the **least** amount?

0 **A** 1,136

0 **B** 1,103

0 **C** 1,154

0 **D** 1,168

5. Which number is greater than 2,012 but less than 2,208?

0 **A** 2,100

0 **B** 2,000

0 **C** 2,210

0 **D** 2,001

Practice 1.B3

I.B Use place value to compare and order whole numbers

1. The list shows the number of play tickets sold by four tour companies.

Company	Tickets
City Tours	1,046
Best Tours	1,604
Eagle Tours	1,406
A-One Tours	1,640

Which company sold the **least** number of tickets?

0 **A** City Tours

0 **B** Best Tours

0 **C** Eagle Tours

0 **D** A-One Tours

2. Which number shows the **greatest** amount?

0 **A** 1,168

0 **B** 1,154

0 **C** 1,130

0 **D** 1,116

3. Which group shows the numbers in order **from greatest to least**?

0 **A** 561 650 643 650

0 **B** 529 643 650 561

0 **C** 650 643 561 529

0 **D** 529 561 643 650

4. Find the number that is between 3,103 and 3,189.

3,103 ______ 3,189

0 **A** 3,198

0 **B** 3,031

0 **C** 3,130

0 **D** 3,195

5. Which number is greater than 1,482 but less than 1,515?

0 **A** 1,467

0 **B** 1,510

0 **C** 1,479

0 **D** 1,520

Practice 1.C1

I.C Round numbers to the nearest ten, hundred, and thousand

1. Alex's class had 3,486 cans to recycle. Rounded to the nearest hundred, the class had—

0 **A** 4,486 cans

0 **B** 4,000 cans

0 **C** 3,500 cans

0 **D** 3,490 cans

2. There are 2,142 books in the school library. Rounded to the nearest ten, there are—

0 **A** 2,200 books

0 **B** 2,150 books

0 **C** 2,140 books

0 **D** 2,100 books

3. Ms. Baker has driven her car 17,219 miles. Rounded to the nearest thousand miles, Ms. Baker has driven—

0 **A** 17,000 miles

0 **B** 17,200 miles

0 **C** 17,300 miles

0 **D** 18,000 miles

4. At Lincoln School, there are 903 students. How many students is this when rounded to the nearest ten?

0 **A** 890

0 **B** 900

0 **C** 910

0 **D** 920

5. Last year 6,219 people visited the City Zoo. Rounded to the nearest hundred, this is—

0 **A** 6,500 people

0 **B** 6,320 people

0 **C** 6,300 people

0 **D** 6,200 people

6. In May, Dr. Jones treated 1,216 people in his office. Rounded to the nearest hundred, how many people did Dr. Jones treat?

0 **A** 1,000

0 **B** 1,100

0 **C** 1,200

0 **D** 1,220

Practice 1.C2

I.C Round numbers to the nearest ten, hundred, and thousand

1. What is 813 rounded to the nearest ten?

0 **A** 800

0 **B** 810

0 **C** 815

0 **D** 820

2. The Tran family drove 864 miles during a trip. Rounded to the nearest hundred, the Tran family drove—

0 **A** 870 miles

0 **B** 900 miles

0 **C** 950 miles

0 **D** 1,000 miles

3. A pool holds 26,342 gallons of water. How many gallons is this rounded to the nearest thousand?

0 **A** 26,400

0 **B** 26,300

0 **C** 26,000

0 **D** 25,000

4. What is 1,749 rounded to the nearest hundred?

0 **A** 1,700

0 **B** 1,750

0 **C** 1,780

0 **D** 1,800

5. What is 13,492 rounded to the nearest thousand?

0 **A** 14,000

0 **B** 13,500

0 **C** 13,400

0 **D** 13,000

6. A truck moved 54,217 pounds of trash to the city dump. How many pounds is this when rounded to the nearest hundred?

0 **A** 54,000

0 **B** 54,200

0 **C** 54,300

0 **D** 55,000

Practice 1.C3

I.C Round numbers to the nearest ten, hundred, and thousand

1. Janice earned 14,094 points on a video game. Rounded to the nearest hundred, how many points did Janice earn?

0 **A** 15,000

0 **B** 14,194

0 **C** 14,100

0 **D** 14,000

2. The best basketball team made 10,293 points in one season. How many points is this rounded to the nearest thousand?

0 **A** 11,000

0 **B** 10,300

0 **C** 10,200

0 **D** 10,000

3. Members of a hiking club walked 5,312 miles in one year. Rounded to the nearest ten miles, the members hiked–

0 **A** 5,400 miles

0 **B** 5,350 miles

0 **C** 5,320 miles

0 **D** 5,310 miles

4. What is 21,591 rounded to the nearest thousand?

0 **A** 21,000

0 **B** 21,500

0 **C** 22,600

0 **D** 22,000

5. What is 7,908 rounded to the nearest ten?

0 **A** 7,900

0 **B** 7,910

0 **C** 7,920

0 **D** 8,000

6. The pet store sold 15,445 pounds of dog food. Rounded to the nearest hundred, this is—

0 **A** 15,000 pounds

0 **B** 15,400 pounds

0 **C** 15,450 pounds

0 **D** 15,500 pounds

Practice 1.D1

***I.D** Use fraction names and symbols to describe and compare fractional parts of whole objects or sets of objects*

1. What fraction of the circles is shaded?

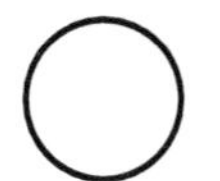   

0 **A** $\frac{2}{4}$

0 **B** $\frac{3}{4}$

0 **C** $\frac{1}{4}$

0 **D** $\frac{1}{2}$

2. Which figure is divided into halves?

0 **A** 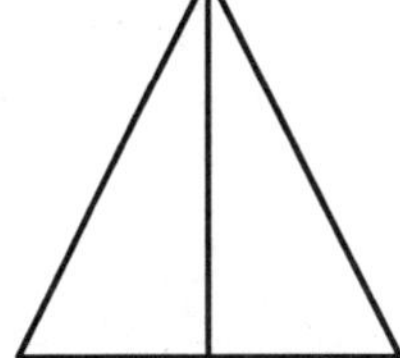

0 **B** 

0 **C** 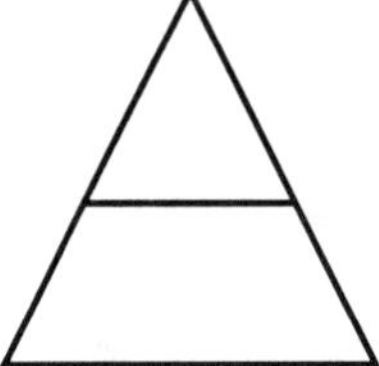

0 **D**

3. What fraction of the rectangles is shaded?

0 **A** $\frac{1}{2}$

0 **B** $\frac{1}{3}$

0 **C** $\frac{2}{5}$

0 **D** $\frac{3}{4}$

4. Which group of circles shows $\frac{3}{4}$ shaded?

0 **A** ○○○●●

0 **B** ●●●○○

0 **C** ○●●●

0 **D** ○○○●

5. Which fraction shows the **greatest** part of a whole?

0 **A** $\frac{3}{4}$

0 **B** $\frac{1}{4}$

0 **C** $\frac{1}{5}$

0 **D** $\frac{1}{6}$

Practice 1.D2

I.D Use fraction names and symbols to describe and compare fractional parts of whole objects or sets of objects

1. What fraction of the rectangle is shaded?

0 **A** $\frac{1}{2}$

0 **B** $\frac{1}{3}$

0 **C** $\frac{2}{3}$

0 **D** $\frac{3}{4}$

2. What fraction of the circles is shaded?

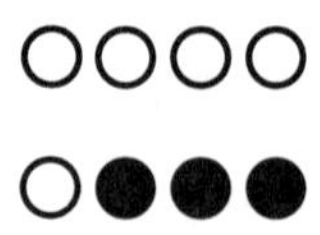

0 **A** $\frac{1}{2}$

0 **B** $\frac{1}{3}$

0 **C** $\frac{1}{8}$

0 **D** $\frac{3}{8}$

3. Which fraction shows how many squares have a letter inside?

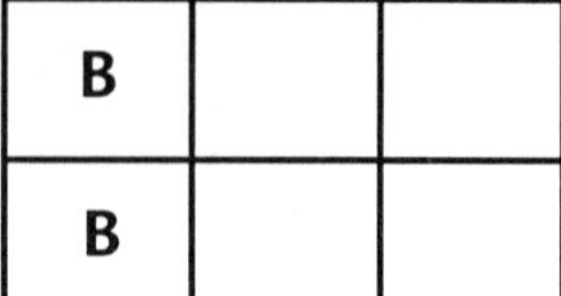

0 **A** $\frac{3}{4}$

0 **B** $\frac{2}{6}$

0 **C** $\frac{1}{6}$

0 **D** $\frac{1}{2}$

4. Which fraction shows how many circles have a number inside?

1 2 3

0 **A** $\frac{1}{4}$

0 **B** $\frac{2}{5}$

0 **C** $\frac{3}{5}$

0 **D** $\frac{3}{4}$

5. Which fraction shows the **smallest** part of a whole?

0 **A** $\frac{2}{3}$

0 **B** $\frac{1}{5}$

0 **C** $\frac{3}{4}$

0 **D** $\frac{1}{2}$

Practice 1.D3

I.D Use fraction names and symbols to describe and compare fractional parts of whole objects or sets of objects

1. Which fraction shows how many of the triangles are shaded?

0 **A** $\frac{2}{7}$

0 **B** $\frac{3}{7}$

0 **C** $\frac{4}{7}$

0 **D** $\frac{6}{7}$

2. Which fraction shows how many boxes have a star inside?

*		*	
	*		*

0 **A** $\frac{1}{8}$

0 **B** $\frac{2}{8}$

0 **C** $\frac{3}{8}$

0 **D** $\frac{4}{8}$

3. Which set shows $\frac{2}{5}$ of the circles shaded?

0 **A** ●●●●○

0 **B** ●●○○○

0 **C** ●●○○●

0 **D** ●○○○○

4. What fraction of the shapes is shaded?

0 **A** $\frac{1}{2}$

0 **B** $\frac{1}{3}$

0 **C** $\frac{4}{9}$

0 **D** $\frac{5}{9}$

5. Which of these is true?

0 **A** $\frac{1}{2} < \frac{1}{3}$

0 **B** $\frac{1}{4} < \frac{1}{5}$

0 **C** $\frac{1}{3} > \frac{1}{6}$

0 **D** $\frac{1}{3} < \frac{1}{5}$

Practice 1.E1

I.E Determine the value of a collection of coins and bills

1. Peggy found the following coins on the sidewalk.

How much money did she find?

0 **A** 54¢

0 **B** 50¢

0 **C** 39¢

0 **D** 25¢

2. A store clerk gave Ann the following coins in change.

How much money did the clerk give to Ann?

0 **A** 95¢

0 **B** 90¢

0 **C** 77¢

0 **D** 41¢

3. How much money would you have if you had 2 dimes, 1 nickel, and 3 pennies?

0 **A** 33¢

0 **B** 28¢

0 **C** 23¢

0 **D** 18¢

4. Tony has 2 one-dollar bills, 1 dime, and 3 nickels. How much money does he have?

0 **A** $1.13

0 **B** $2.04

0 **C** $2.13

0 **D** $2.25

5. Ajay paid for a newspaper with these coins.

How much did he pay for the newspaper?

0 **A** 70¢

0 **B** 55¢

0 **C** 50¢

0 **D** 45¢

Practice 1.E2

I.E Determine the value of a collection of coins and bills

1. Jon paid for a soda with the following coins.

How much did he pay?

0 **A** 45¢

0 **B** 48¢

0 **C** 50¢

0 **D** 65¢

2. Mrs. Tanner found these coins.

How much money did she find?

0 **A** 40¢

0 **B** 41¢

0 **C** 46¢

0 **D** 48¢

3. How much money would you have if you had 2 quarters, 2 dimes, and 2 nickels?

0 **A** 70¢

0 **B** 75¢

0 **C** 80¢

0 **D** 90¢

4. Molly has 4 one-dollar bills, 3 nickels, and 2 pennies. How much money does she have?

0 **A** $4.07

0 **B** $4.17

0 **C** $4.32

0 **D** $4.78

5. Shirley paid for a pen with these coins.

How much did she pay for the pen?

0 **A** 61¢

0 **B** 79¢

0 **C** $1.00

0 **D** $1.10

Practice 1.E3

I.E Determine the value of a collection of coins and bills

1. The store clerk gave Annie these coins in change.

How much money did Annie get?

0 **A** 35¢

0 **B** 37¢

0 **C** 40¢

0 **D** 52¢

2. Ed's mother gave him 2 dimes, 3 nickels, and 8 pennies. How much money is that?

0 **A** 43¢

0 **B** 48¢

0 **C** 58¢

0 **D** 38¢

3. How much money would you have if you had 3 one-dollar bills, 4 nickels, and 7 pennies?

0 **A** $3.47

0 **B** $3.39

0 **C** $3.27

0 **D** $3.11

4. For a magazine, Myra gave the clerk 2 one-dollar bills, 2 quarters, and 5 pennies. How much did the magazine cost?

0 **A** $2.70

0 **B** $2.55

0 **C** $2.65

0 **D** $2.50

5. Nick found these coins in his desk.

How much money did he find?

0 **A** 85¢

0 **B** 75¢

0 **C** 70¢

0 **D** 62¢

Practice 1.F1

I.F Read, write, compare, and order decimals expressed to hundredths

1. Which decimal shows the **greatest** amount?

0 **A** 2.01

0 **B** 2.5

0 **C** 2.15

0 **D** 0.25

2. Which one shows the numbers in order **from least to greatest**?

0 **A** 3.02 3.12 3.22 3.2

0 **B** 3.2 3.22 3.12 3.02

0 **C** 3.22 3.12 3.2 3.02

0 **D** 3.02 3.12 3.2 3.22

3. The teacher added five tenths of a point to Dawn's grade. How is this number written?

0 **A** 5.0

0 **B** 0.05

0 **C** 0.5

0 **D** 1.5

4. Which number tells how much is shaded?

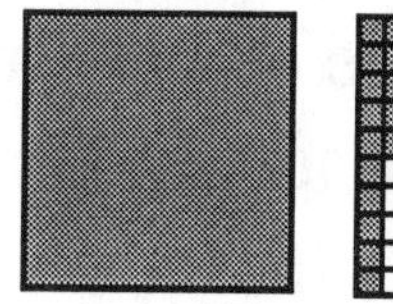

0 **A** 11.5

0 **B** 10.15

0 **C** 1.15

0 **D** 1.1

5. Which one shows the numbers in order **from greatest to least**?

0 **A** 13.0 1.13 1.3 1.03

0 **B** 1.13 1.3 13.0 1.03

0 **C** 13.0 1.3 1.13 1.03

0 **D** 1.03 1.13 1.3 13.0

6. Diana has 42¢. How is this amount written as a decimal?

0 **A** $4.02

0 **B** $4.20

0 **C** $0.42

0 **D** $2.40

Practice 1.F2

I.F Read, write, compare, and order decimals expressed to hundredths

1. Bobby won the contest by jumping one and two tenths of an inch higher than Eric. How is this number written?

0 **A** 0.12

0 **B** 2.1

0 **C** 1.02

0 **D** 1.2

2. Which one shows the numbers in order from **least to greatest**?

0 **A** 35 30.5 3.5 3.05

0 **B** 3.05 3.5 30.5 35

0 **C** 30.5 3.05 35 3.5

0 **D** 3.05 35 3.4 3.05

3. Tucker has 56¢. How is this amount written as a decimal?

0 **A** $0.56

0 **B** $5.06

0 **C** $5.60

0 **D** $6.50

4. Which decimal tells how much is shaded?

 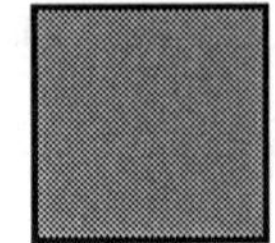 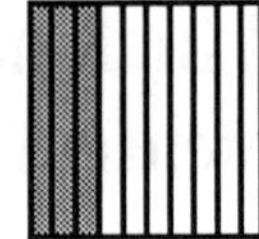

0 **A** 20.3

0 **B** 20.03

0 **C** 2.3

0 **D** 2.03

5. How do you read the number 2.15?

0 **A** two hundred fifteen tenths

0 **B** two and fifteen tenths

0 **C** two and fifteen hundredths

0 **D** two hundred, fifteen

6. Which one shows the numbers in order from **greatest to least**?

0 **A** 0.45 0.1 0.17 0.12

0 **B** 0.45 0.17 0.12 0.1

0 **C** 0.1 0.12 0.17 0.45

0 **D** 0.17 0.45 0.1 0.12

Practice 1.F3

I.F Read, write, compare, and order decimals expressed to hundredths

1. Which number shows the **least** amount?

0 **A** 1.25

0 **B** 12.5

0 **C** 12.05

0 **D** 1.52

2. Which number shows the **greatest** amount?

0 **A** 3.03

0 **B** 0.33

0 **C** 3.13

0 **D** 3.3

3. Which one shows the numbers in order from **greatest to least**?

0 **A** 4.05 4.15 4.5 4.51

0 **B** 4.05 4.51 4.5 4.15

0 **C** 4.51 4.5 4.15 4.05

0 **D** 4.15 4.05 4.51 4.5

4. How do you read the number 1.05?

0 **A** one and five tenths

0 **B** one hundred five tenths

0 **C** one hundred five

0 **D** one and five hundredths

5. Which picture shows 2.11?

0 **A**

0 **B**

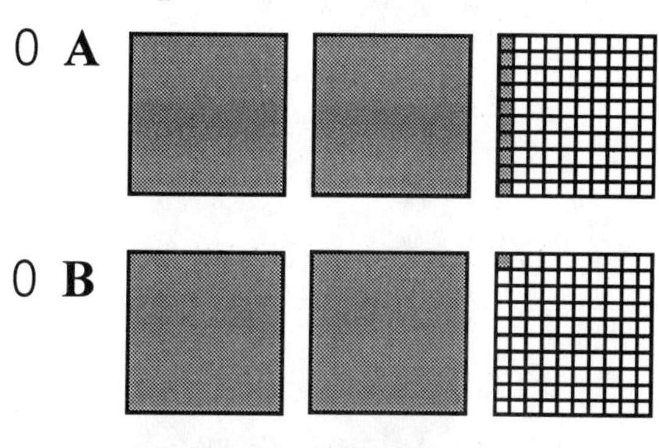

0 **C**

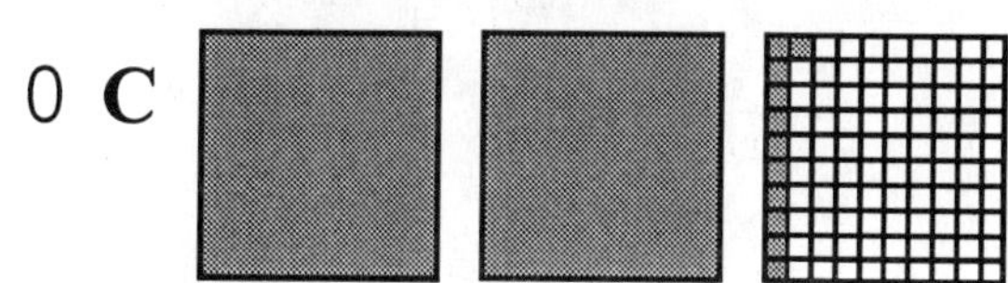

0 **D**

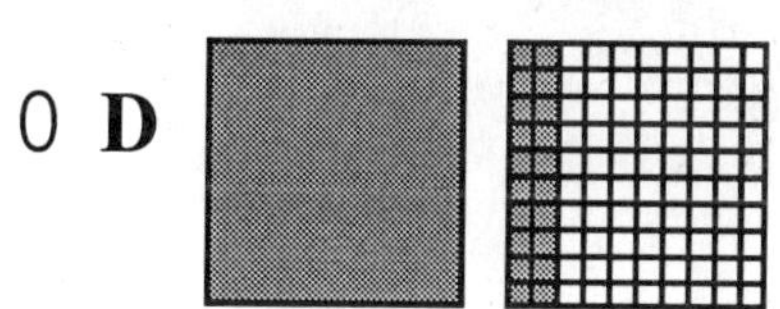

Notes

Mathematical Relations, Functions, & Algebraic Concepts

II. Demonstrate an understanding of mathematical relations, functions, and other algebraic concepts

A. Identify and extend whole-number and geometric patterns to make predictions and solve problems
B. Identify patterns in number sentences (fact families)
C. Solve problems involving numeric equations or inequalities
D. Identify patterns in a table of related number pairs based on a real-life situation and generate or extend the table

Notes

Objective 2: Pretest

II.A Identify and extend whole-number and geometric patterns to make predictions and solve problems (1-6)

1. Which number goes in the empty space in this number pattern?

88, _____, 84, 82, 80

0 **A** 89

0 **B** 87

0 **C** 86

0 **D** 85

2. Which number goes in the empty space of this number pattern?

12, 9, 6, _____, 0

0 **A** 7

0 **B** 5

0 **C** 4

0 **D** 3

3. Which number goes in the empty space of this number pattern?

633, 638, 643, _____, 653

0 **A** 650

0 **B** 649

0 **C** 648

0 **D** 645

4. How many stars should be in box 4?

1 ☆☆☆☆☆

2

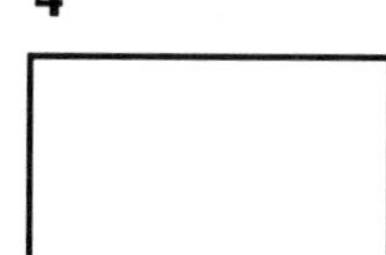

3 ☆☆☆☆☆ ☆☆☆☆☆ ☆☆☆☆☆

4

0 **A** 4

0 **B** 10

0 **C** 18

0 **D** 20

5. What shape goes in the empty space?

○ ○ ◁ ○ ○ ▭ ○ ___ ◁

0 **A** ▭

0 **B** ◁

0 **C** ○

0 **D** ⬭

6. Tina had 10 candy bars. She ate 2 bars every day. How many candy bars did she have after the third day?

0 **A** 8

0 **B** 7

0 **C** 6

0 **D** 4

II.B Identify patterns in number sentences (7-16)

7. Which number belongs in the box?

22 – ☐ = 17

0 **A** 15

0 **B** 12

0 **C** 7

0 **D** 5

8. Which sign belongs in the box?

4 ☐ 6 = 24

0 **A** +

0 **B** –

0 **C** ÷

0 **D** x

9. Which number sentence belongs in the same family of facts as 9 + 7 = 16?

0 **A** 9 – 7 = 2

0 **B** 16 – 9 = 7

0 **C** 9 x 7 = 63

0 **D** 8 + 8 = 16

10. Which names the same number as 6 + 7 + 3?

0 **A** 7 – 6 + 3

0 **B** 7 x 6 + 3

0 **C** 3 + 7 + 6

0 **D** 7 x 6 x 3

11. Which number sentence is NOT in the same family of facts as 9 x 2 = 18?

0 **A** 18 ÷ 2 = 9

0 **B** 18 ÷ 9 = 2

0 **C** 2 x 9 = 18

0 **D** 9 + 2 = 11

12. Which sign makes this number sentence true?

9 ☐ 3 = 15 + 12

0 **A** +

0 **B** –

0 **C** ÷

0 **D** x

13. Which number sentence is in the same family of facts as 20 – 13 = 7?

0 **A** 20 + 13 + 7 = 40

0 **B** 20 + 13 = 33

0 **C** 20 + 7 = 27

0 **D** 13 + 7 = 20

14. Which number sentence is true?

0 **A** 8 + 2 < 9

0 **B** 12 – 4 > 10

0 **C** 7 x 2 > 12

0 **D** 12 ÷ 4 < 2

15. Which number sentence could you use to check the answer for 19 + 3 = 22?

0 **A** 22 – 3 = 19

0 **B** 22 + 3 = 25

0 **C** 19 – 3 = 16

0 **D** 22 + 19 = 41

16. Which number would make this number sentence correct?

8 – 2 + 3 = 10 – 3 + ☐

0 **A** 5

0 **B** 4

0 **C** 3

0 **D** 2

II.C Solve problems involving numeric equations or inequalities (17–21)

17. Terri collected 8 rocks in June and 16 rocks in July. Which number sentence shows how many more rocks Terri collected in July than in June?

0 **A** 16 + 8 = 24

0 **B** 16 – 8 = 8

0 **C** 16 x 8 = 128

0 **D** 16 ÷ 8 = 2

18. Jerry has 12 pieces of candy. He wants to give each of his 3 friends the same amount of candy. Which number sentence shows how many pieces of candy each friend will get?

0 **A** $12 + 3 = 15$

0 **B** $12 - 3 = 9$

0 **C** $12 \times 3 = 36$

0 **D** $12 \div 3 = 4$

19. Rick bought 4 boxes of pens. There were 8 pens in each box. Which number sentence shows how many pens Rick bought?

0 **A** $8 - 4 = 4$

0 **B** $8 \div 4 = 2$

0 **C** $8 \times 4 = 32$

0 **D** $8 + 4 = 12$

20. Karl had 26 baseball cards. He bought 10 more cards from Jesse and 8 more cards from Mary. Which number sentence shows how many cards Karl had in all?

0 **A** $26 - 10 - 8 = 8$

0 **B** $26 + 10 - 8 = 28$

0 **C** $26 + 10 + 8 = 44$

0 **D** $26 + 8 - 10 = 24$

21. Every student who reads 5 books wins 3 candy bars. In Mrs. West's class, 5 students read 5 books each. Which number sentence shows how many candy bars they won in all?

0 **A** $6 \times 3 = 18$

0 **B** $5 \times 3 = 15$

0 **C** $6 \times 5 = 30$

0 **D** $6 + 5 = 11$

II.D Identify patterns in a table of related number pairs based on a real-life situation and generate or extend the table (22–25)

22. The table shows how many pieces of candy Kim can buy for each dime she spends. What number should go in the blank box on the table ?

Dimes	Pieces of Candy
1	2
2	4
3	6
4	
5	10

0 **A** 12
0 **B** 10
0 **C** 8
0 **D** 6

23. The table shows how many inches of ribbon Pam uses on the packages she wraps. What number should go in the blank box on the table?

Ribbon	Packages
10 in.	1
20 in.	2
	3
40 in.	4
50 in.	5

0 **A** 10 in.
0 **B** 15 in.
0 **C** 25 in.
0 **D** 30 in.

24. Mr. Watt's class checks the outside temperature every hour. The table shows the temperature for 5 straight hours. If the temperature goes up the same amount each hour, what number should go in the blank box?

Time	Temperature
9:00	74°F
10:00	77°F
11:00	
12:00	83°F
1:00	86°F

0 **A** 78°F

0 **B** 80°F

0 **C** 82°F

0 **D** 85°F

25. The table shows how much a soft drink company charges for cases of its drinks. What number should go in the blank box on the table?

Cases	Cost
1	$12
2	$24
3	$36
4	
5	$60

0 **A** $38

0 **B** $40

0 **C** $44

0 **D** $48

Practice 2.A1

II.A Identify and extend whole-number and geometric patterns to make predictions and solve problems

1. Which number goes in the empty space in this number pattern?

445, 448, _____, 454

0 **A** 453

0 **B** 452

0 **C** 451

0 **D** 449

2. Which number goes in the empty space in this number pattern?

2, 4, 8, 16, 32, _____

0 **A** 33

0 **B** 36

0 **C** 42

0 **D** 64

3. Which number goes in the empty space in this number pattern?

480, 470, 460, _____, 440

0 **A** 490

0 **B** 475

0 **C** 455

0 **D** 450

4. The first house on Elm Street has the number 222. If the house numbers jump by 4, what is the number on the **fourth** house?

0 **A** 220

0 **B** 224

0 **C** 234

0 **D** 238

5. What shape goes in the empty space?

○ ◁ ▭ ○ ◁ ___ ○ ◁ ▭

0 **A** ▭

0 **B** ◁

0 **C** ○

0 **D** □

Practice 2.A2

II.A Identify and extend whole-number and geometric patterns to make predictions and solve problems

1. Which number goes in the empty space in this number pattern?

632, 637, 642, _____, 652

0 **A** 645

0 **B** 646

0 **C** 647

0 **D** 650

2. Which number goes in the empty space in this number pattern?

54, 45, 36, 27, _____, 9

0 **A** 15

0 **B** 18

0 **C** 25

0 **D** 30

3. Which number goes in the empty space in this number pattern?

3, 6, 9, _____, 15

0 **A** 10

0 **B** 11

0 **C** 12

0 **D** 13

4. Cary put 4 blue beads on the first bracelet she made, 8 blue beads on the second bracelet, and 12 blue beads on the third bracelet. How many blue beads did she probably put on the **fifth** bracelet she made?

0 **A** 5

0 **B** 16

0 **C** 18

0 **D** 20

5. How many stars should be in box 4?

1

☆ ☆ ☆ ☆

2

☆ ☆ ☆ ☆ ☆
☆ ☆ ☆ ☆

3

4

0 **A** 16

0 **B** 18

0 **C** 19

0 **D** 20

Practice 2.A3

II.A Identify and extend whole-number and geometric patterns to make predictions and solve problems

1. Which number goes in the empty space in this number pattern?

346, 340, 334, _____, 322

0 **A** 335

0 **B** 328

0 **C** 326

0 **D** 330

2. Which number goes in the empty space in this number pattern?

12, 14, 18, 24, _____, 42

0 **A** 28

0 **B** 30

0 **C** 32

0 **D** 36

3. Which number goes in the empty space in this number pattern?

36, 30, _____, 18, 12

0 **A** 28

0 **B** 26

0 **C** 24

0 **D** 20

4. Mr. Gonzalez uses 12 gallons of gas a week. How many gallons of gas will he have used at the end of 4 weeks?

0 **A** 50

0 **B** 48

0 **C** 40

0 **D** 16

5. What shape goes in the empty space?

0 **A**

0 **B**

0 **C**

0 **D**

Practice 2.B1

II.B Identify patterns in number sentences

1. Which number belongs in the box?

53 – ☐ = 46

0 **A** 99

0 **B** 17

0 **C** 9

0 **D** 7

2. Which sign belongs in the box?

45 ☐ 9 = 5

0 **A** +

0 **B** –

0 **C** ÷

0 **D** x

3. Which number sentence belongs in the same family of facts as 8 x 3 = 24?

0 **A** 8 + 3 = 11

0 **B** 24 + 3 = 27

0 **C** 24 ÷ 3 = 8

0 **D** 24 – 8 = 16

4. Which names the same number as 9 + 3 + 4?

0 **A** 4 + 3 + 9

0 **B** 9 – 4 + 3

0 **C** 9 x 3 x 4

0 **D** 9 x 3 – 4

5. Which number sentence is NOT in the same family of facts as 5 x 9 = 45?

0 **A** 5 + 9 = 14

0 **B** 9 x 5 = 45

0 **C** 45 ÷ 9 = 5

0 **D** 45 ÷ 5 = 9

6. Which number sentence could you use to check the answer for 12 x 4 = 48?

0 **A** 12 + 4 = 16

0 **B** 12 ÷ 4 = 3

0 **C** 48 + 4 = 52

0 **D** 48 ÷ 4 = 12

Practice 2.B2

II.B Identify patterns in number sentences

1. Which number belongs in the box?

☐ x 7 = 63

0 **A** 7

0 **B** 8

0 **C** 9

0 **D** 10

2. Which sign belongs in the box?

48 ☐ 8 = 6

0 **A** +

0 **B** –

0 **C** ÷

0 **D** x

3. Which number sentence belongs in the same family of facts as 56 ÷ 8 = 7?

0 **A** 56 + 7 = 63

0 **B** 56 – 7 = 49

0 **C** 8 + 7 = 15

0 **D** 8 x 7 = 56

4. Which number sentence is true?

0 **A** 28 – 19 < 8

0 **B** 7 x 3 > 18

0 **C** 8 ÷ 5 > 5

0 **D** 7 + 8 > 20

5. Which number sentence is NOT in the same family of facts as 24 + 48 = 72?

0 **A** 72 – 48 = 24

0 **B** 72 – 24 = 48

0 **C** 48 + 24 = 72

0 **D** 72 + 24 = 96

6. Which number sentence could you use to check the answer for 86 – 28 = 58?

0 **A** 58 + 28 = 86

0 **B** 58 – 28 = 30

0 **C** 86 + 28 = 114

0 **D** 86 + 58 = 144

Practice 2.B3

II.B Identify patterns in number sentences

1. Which number would make the following number sentence true?

$\square + 46 > 58$

0 **A** 8

0 **B** 9

0 **C** 12

0 **D** 14

2. Which sign belongs in the box?

$16 + 12 \ \square \ 30$

0 **A** $>$

0 **B** $=$

0 **C** $\geq$

0 **D** $<$

3. Which number sentence belongs in the same family of facts as 23 + 19 = 42?

0 **A** 42 + 19 = 61

0 **B** 23 – 19 = 4

0 **C** 42 – 23 = 19

0 **D** 42 + 23 = 65

4. Which names the same number as 2 x 1 x 4?

0 **A** 2 + 1 + 4

0 **B** 4 x 2 x 1

0 **C** 4 x 2 + 1

0 **D** 2 + 1 x 4

5. Which number sentence is NOT in the same family of facts as 12 x 3 = 36?

0 **A** 36 ÷ 3 = 12

0 **B** 36 ÷ 12 = 3

0 **C** 36 – 3 = 33

0 **D** 3 x 12 = 36

6. Which number makes the following number sentence true?

$6 \times 6 = \square - 4$

0 **A** 40

0 **B** 36

0 **C** 12

0 **D** 8

Practice 2.C1

II.C Solve problems involving numeric equations or inequalities

1. On Monday, 42 students ordered candy. On Tuesday, 15 more students ordered candy. Which number sentence shows how many students ordered candy?

0 **A** 42 – 15 = 27

0 **B** 42 + 15 = 57

0 **C** 27 + 15 = 42

0 **D** 57 + 15 = 72

2. Betty hiked 17 miles during May. She hiked 32 miles during June. Which number sentence shows how many more miles Betty hiked in June than in May?

0 **A** 32 + 17 = 49

0 **B** 49 – 32 = 17

0 **C** 17 + 15 = 32

0 **D** 32 – 17 = 15

3. Every player who earned 3 points during the game won 4 tokens. In Franny's class, 8 students earned 3 points. Which number sentence shows how many tokens the students won?

0 **A** 8 x 3 = 24

0 **B** 8 + 3 + 4 = 15

0 **C** 8 x 4 = 32

0 **D** 4 x 3 = 12

4. Kate has 48 pennies. She wants to put the same number of pennies in 6 cups. Which number sentence shows how many pennies Kate will put in each cup?

0 **A** 48 + 6 = 54

0 **B** 48 ÷ 6 = 8

0 **C** 48 – 6 = 42

0 **D** 54 – 8 = 46

Practice 2.C2

II.C Solve problems involving numeric equations or inequalities

1. Mrs. Taylor needed 18 students to help on the playground. Only 6 girls and 7 boys came to help her. Mrs. Taylor needed more helpers. Which number sentence goes with this problem?

0 **A** 18 + 7 = 25

0 **B** 18 + 6 = 24

0 **C** 6 + 7 < 18

0 **D** 6 + 7 > 12

2. Madison worked on the computer for 47 minutes. Austin worked on the computer for 38 minutes. Which number sentence shows how many more minutes Madison worked on the computer than Austin?

0 **A** 47 + 38 = 85

0 **B** 85 – 38 = 47

0 **C** 9 + 47 = 56

0 **D** 47 – 38 = 9

3. Gracie is making cookies for her party. She wants each guest to have 3 cookies. She needs cookies for 9 people. Which number sentence shows how many cookies Gracie must make?

0 **A** 9 x 3 = 27

0 **B** 9 + 3 = 12

0 **C** 9 ÷ 3 = 3

0 **D** 9 – 3 = 6

4. Doug has 56 trading cards. He wants to put the same number of cards on 8 pages of a book. Which number sentence shows how many cards Doug will put on each page?

0 **A** 56 + 8 = 64

0 **B** 56 ÷ 8 = 7

0 **C** 56 – 8 = 48

0 **D** 64 – 8 = 56

Practice 2.C3

II.C Solve problems involving numeric equations or inequalities

1. Zach earned 46 points in a math game. He lost 13 points because he did not do his homework. Which number sentence shows how many points Zach had in the end?

0 **A** $46 + 13 = 59$

0 **B** $46 - 13 = 33$

0 **C** $33 + 46 = 79$

0 **D** $33 - 13 = 20$

2. Suzanne is saving money for a new radio. The radio costs $57. Suzanne has saved $29. Which number sentence shows how much more she must save?

0 **A** \$57 + \$29 = \$86

0 **B** \$86 – \$29 = \$57

0 **C** \$28 + \$57 = \$85

0 **D** \$57 – \$29 = \$28

3. Kathy made 24 cookies. She wants to give her 4 brothers the same number of cookies. Which number sentence shows how many cookies each brother can have?

0 **A** $24 + 4 > 22$

0 **B** $24 - 4 < 28$

0 **C** $24 \div 4 = 6$

0 **D** $24 + 4 = 28$

4. Max earned $15 for cutting the grass. He earned $8 for mopping the floor. Which number sentence shows how much Max earned?

0 **A** \$15 – \$8 = \$7

0 **B** \$15 + \$8 = \$23

0 **C** \$15 x \$8 = \$120

0 **D** \$23 + \$15 = \$38

Practice 2.D1

II.D Identify patterns in a table of related number pairs based on a real-life situation and generate or extend the table

1. The table shows how much paper students will use for an art project. What number of sheets should go in the blank box on the table?

Number of Students	Paper Needed
3	5 sheets
6	10 sheets
9	
12	20 sheets
15	25 sheets

0 **A** 10

0 **B** 12

0 **C** 15

0 **D** 22

2. Mrs. Kennedy must order roses to make decorations for a party. She will use the table to find out how many roses she must order. What number should go in the blank box on the table?

Number of Decorations	Number of Roses
3	6
6	12
9	18
12	
15	30

0 **A** 28

0 **B** 24

0 **C** 20

0 **D** 12

Practice 2.D2

***II.D** Identify patterns in a table of related number pairs based on a real-life situation and generate or extend the table*

1. Liz is making toy spiders for her little brother. The table shows how many wire legs she will use for the spiders. What number should go in the blank box on the table?

Number of Spiders	Number of Legs
1	8
2	
3	24
4	32
5	40

0 **A** 18

0 **B** 16

0 **C** 14

0 **D** 12

2. Kiran is making punch for a party. The table shows how many guests Kiran can serve with the bowls of punch he makes. What number should go in the blank box on the table?

Number of Guests	Bowls of Punch
12	1
24	2
36	3
	4
60	5

0 **A** 40

0 **B** 44

0 **C** 48

0 **D** 50

Practice 2.D3

***II.D** Identify patterns in a table of related number pairs based on a real-life situation and generate or extend the table*

1. The table shows how much flour a bakery uses to make pretzels. What number should go in the blank box on the table?

Pounds of Flour	Boxes of Pretzels
2	15
4	
6	45
8	60
10	75

0 **A** 15

0 **B** 25

0 **C** 30

0 **D** 35

2. The table shows how much a candy store charges for boxes of candy. What number should go in the blank box on the table?

Boxes of Candy	Cost of Candy
12	$25
24	$50
36	
48	$100
60	$125

0 **A** $48

0 **B** $55

0 **C** $60

0 **D** $75

Geometric Properties/ Relationships

III. Demonstrate an understanding of geometric properties and relationships

A. Name, describe, and compare shapes and solids, using formal geometric vocabulary
B. Identify congruent shapes
C. Identify lines of symmetry in shapes
D. Locate and name points on a number line, using whole numbers and simple fractions

Notes

Objective 3: Pretest

III.A Name, describe, and compare shapes and solids, using formal geometric vocabulary (1-6)

1. Which is a picture of a square?

0 **A** 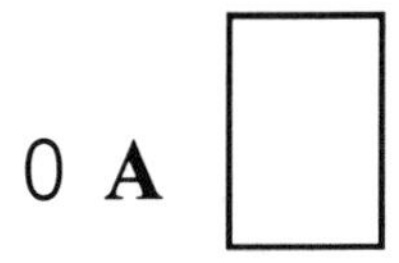

0 **B** 

0 **C** 

0 **D** 

2. How many sides does this shape have?

0 **A** 2

0 **B** 3

0 **C** 4

0 **D** 5

3. Which letter is inside the rectangle?

0 **A** T

0 **B** S

0 **C** R

0 **D** Q

4. Which is a picture of a cube?

0 **A** 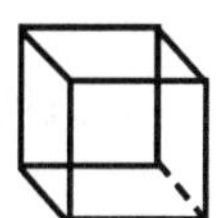

0 **B** 

0 **C** 

0 **D** 

5. How many angles does this shape have?

0 **A** 2

0 **B** 3

0 **C** 4

0 **D** 6

6. What is the correct name for this shape?

0 **A** square

0 **B** circle

0 **C** rectangle

0 **D** triangle

III.B Identify congruent shapes (7-10)

7. Which shape is congruent to this one?

0 **A**

0 **B**

0 **C**

0 **D**

8. Which pair of shapes is congruent?

0 **A**

0 **B**

0 **C**

0 **D**

9. Which shape is congruent to this one?

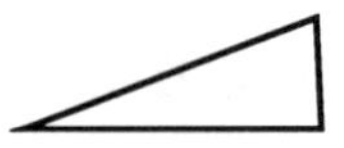

0 **A**

0 **B** 

0 **C**

0 **D**

10. Which pair of shapes is congruent?

0 **A**

0 **B**

0 **C** 

0 **D**

III.C Identify lines of symmetry in shapes (11-14)

11. On which shape does the dotted line show a line of symmetry?

0 **A** 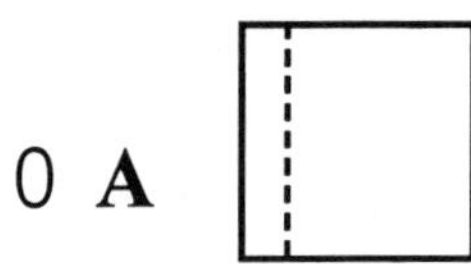

0 **B** 

0 **C** 

0 **D** 

12. Which shape does NOT have at least one line of symmetry?

0 **A** 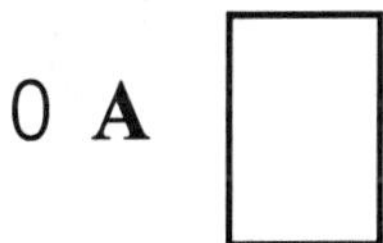

0 **B**

0 **C**

0 **D**

13. On which shape does the dotted line show a line of symmetry?

0 **A** 

0 **B** 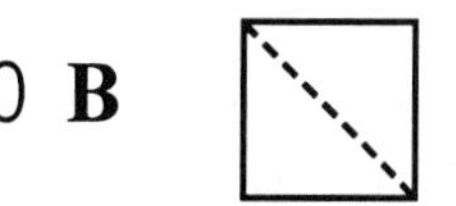

0 **C** 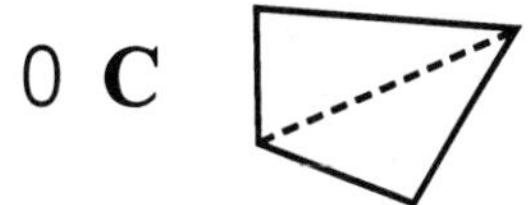

0 **D** 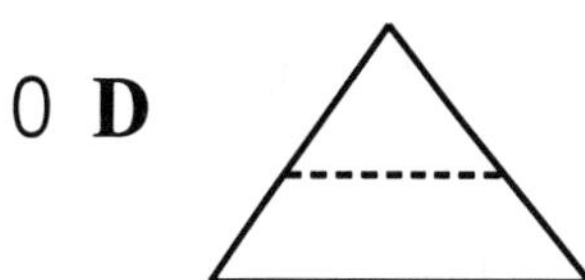

14. Which shape has at least one line of symmetry?

0 **A** 

0 **B** 

0 **C** 

0 **D** 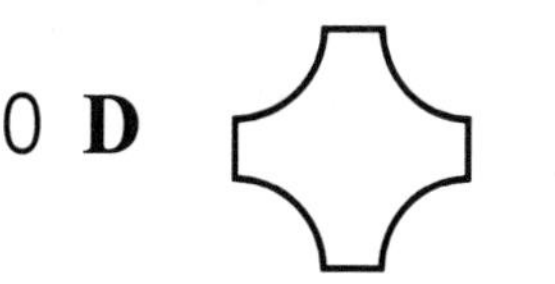

III.D Locate and name points on a number line using whole numbers and simple fractions (15-18)

15. Which number line has a star on the whole number that is between 29 and 31?

0 **A** 

0 **B** 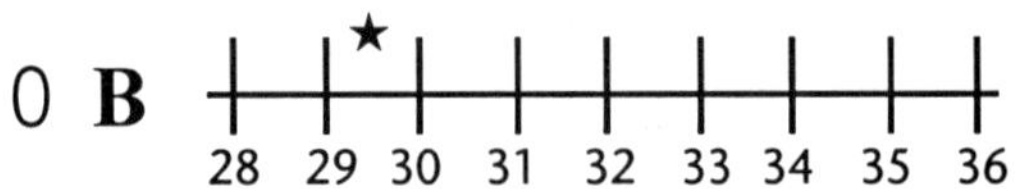

0 **C** 

0 **D** 

16. What number belongs where you see the letter D?

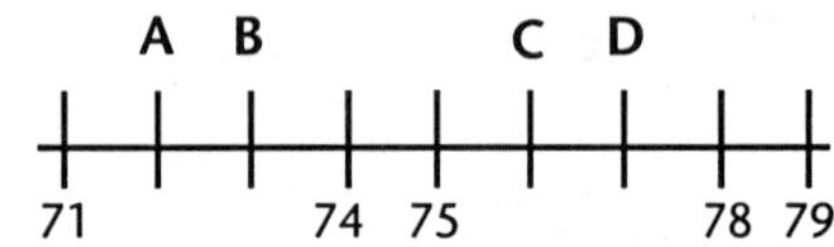

0 **A** 72

0 **B** 73

0 **C** 75

0 **D** 77

17. Which number line has a star on $14\frac{1}{2}$?

0 **A** 

0 **B** 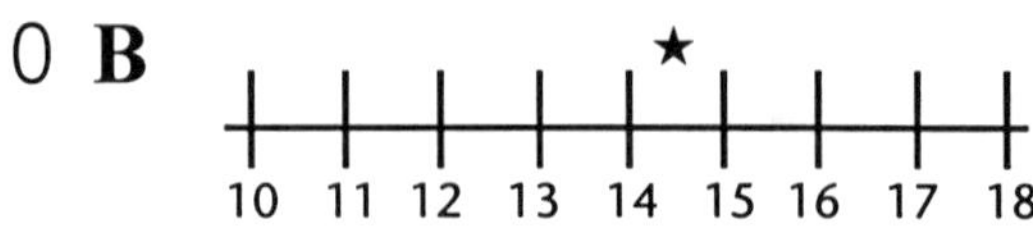

0 **C** 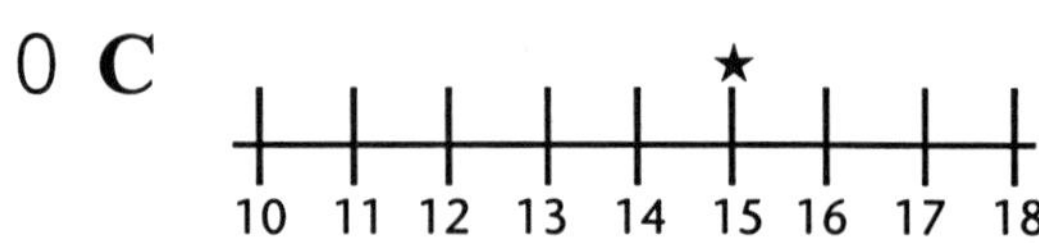

0 **D** 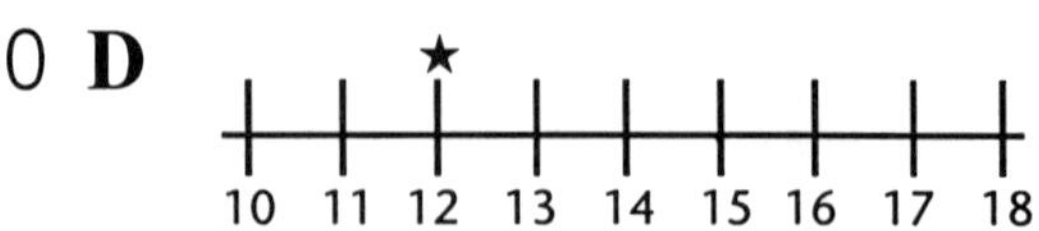

18. What number belongs where you see the letter T?

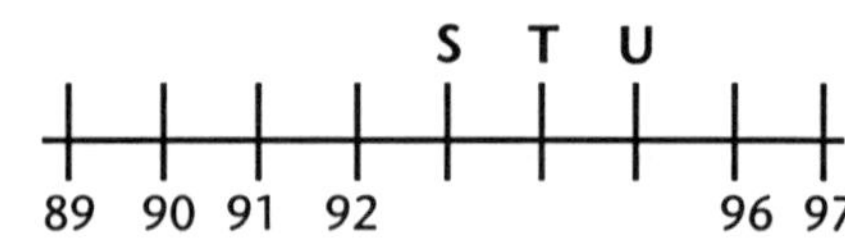

0 **A** 96

0 **B** 95

0 **C** 94

0 **D** 93

Practice 3.A1

III.A Name, describe, and compare shapes and solids using formal geometric vocabulary

1. Which is a picture of a triangle?

0 **A**

0 **B**

0 **C**

0 **D**

2. How many angles does this shape have?

0 **A** 3

0 **B** 5

0 **C** 6

0 **D** 8

3. Which letter is inside the circle?

0 **A** E

0 **B** F

0 **C** G

0 **D** H

4. Which is a picture of a sphere?

0 **A** 

0 **B**

0 **C** 

0 **D**

5. How many sides does this shape have?

0 **A** 2

0 **B** 3

0 **C** 5

0 **D** 6

6. What is the correct name for this shape?

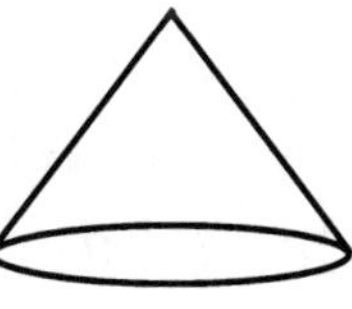

0 **A** cube

0 **B** cone

0 **C** square

0 **D** triangle

Practice 3.A2

III.A Name, describe, and compare shapes and solids using formal geometric vocabulary

1. Which is a picture of a cylinder?

0 **A** 

0 **B** 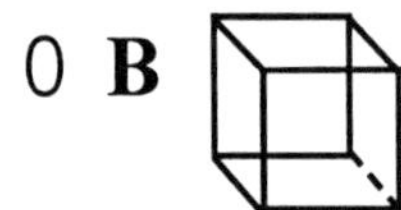

0 **C** 

0 **D** 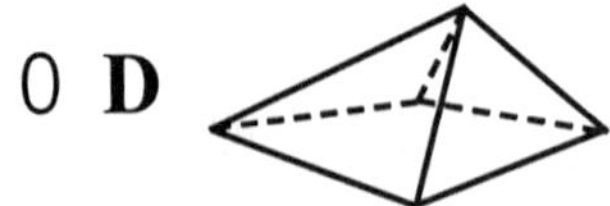

2. What is the correct name for this shape?

0 **A** square

0 **B** cube

0 **C** triangle

0 **D** rectangle

3. How many sides does this shape have?

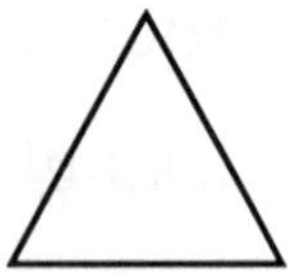

0 **A** 6

0 **B** 4

0 **C** 3

0 **D** 2

4. Which is a picture of a cone?

0 **A**

0 **B**

0 **C**

0 **D**

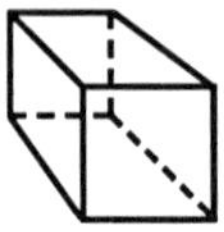

5. Which one shows a triangle inside a square?

0 **A**

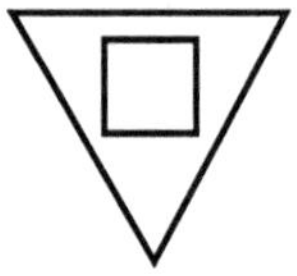

0 **B**

0 **C**

0 **D**

Practice 3.A3

III.A Name, describe, and compare shapes and solids using formal geometric vocabulary

1. What is the correct name for this shape?

0 **A** cone

0 **B** cylinder

0 **C** rectangle

0 **D** pyramid

2. A can of soup has the shape of a—

0 **A** cube

0 **B** cylinder

0 **C** cone

0 **D** triangle

3. What is the total number of angles in these two shapes?

0 **A** 7

0 **B** 6

0 **C** 4

0 **D** 2

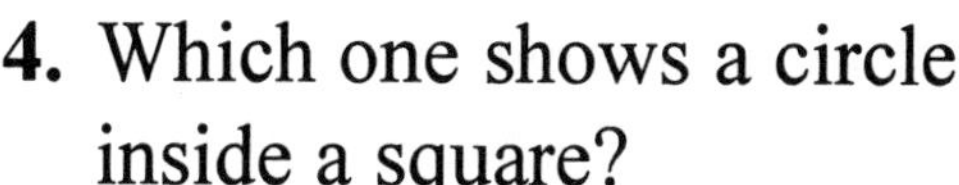

4. Which one shows a circle inside a square?

0 **A**

0 **B**

0 **C**

0 **D**

5. Which one is NOT a triangle?

0 **A**

0 **B**

0 **C**

0 **D**

Practice 3.B1

III.B Identify congruent shapes

1. Which shape is congruent to this one?

0 **A**

0 **B**

0 **C**

0 **D**

2. Which pair of shapes is congruent?

0 **A** 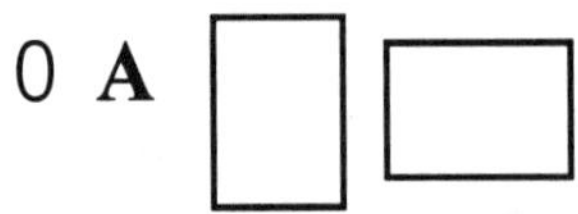

0 **B** 

0 **C** 

0 **D** 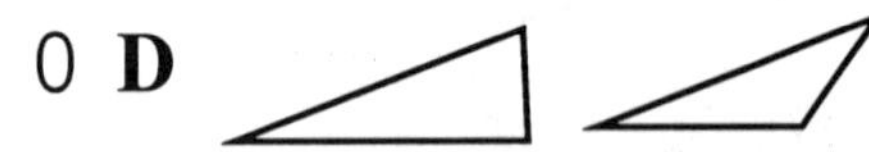

3. Which shape is congruent to this one?

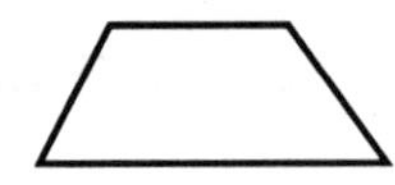

0 **A**

0 **B**

0 **C**

0 **D**

4. Which pair of shapes is NOT congruent?

0 **A** 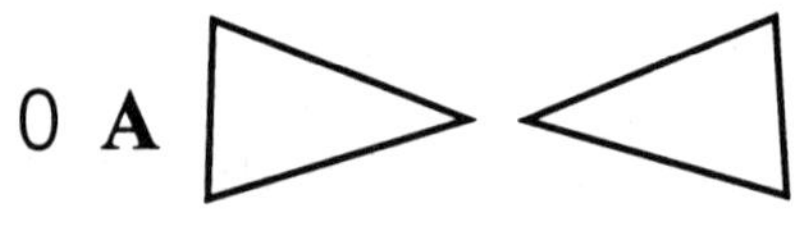

0 **B**

0 **C**

0 **D**

Practice 3.B2

III.B Identify congruent shapes

1. Which shape is congruent to this one?

0 **A** 

0 **B** 

0 **C** 

0 **D** 

2. Which pair of figures is congruent?

0 **A** 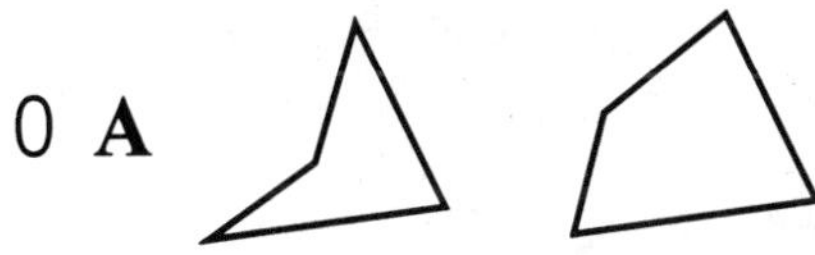

0 **B** 

0 **C** 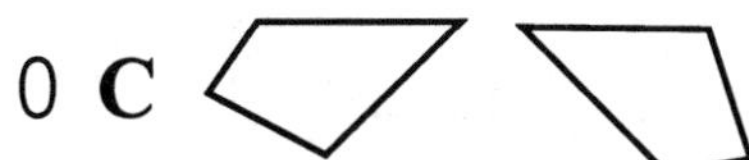

0 **D** 

3. Which shape is congruent to this one?

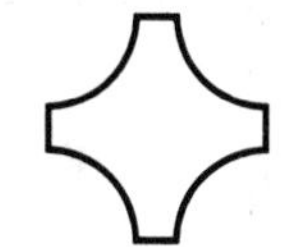

0 **A**

0 **B** 

0 **C**

0 **D** 

4. Which pair of shapes is NOT congruent?

0 **A**

0 **B** 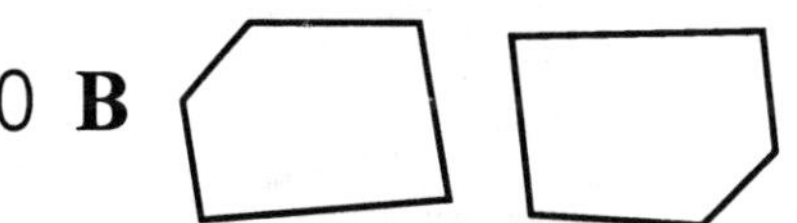

0 **C**

0 **D** 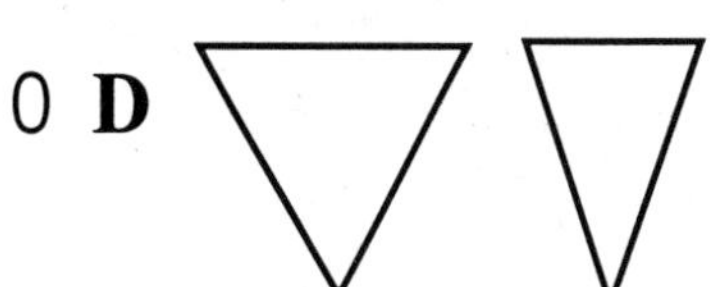

Practice 3.B3

III.B Identify congruent shapes

1. Which shape is congruent to this one?

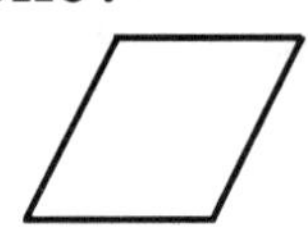

0 **A** 

0 **B** 

0 **C** 

0 **D** 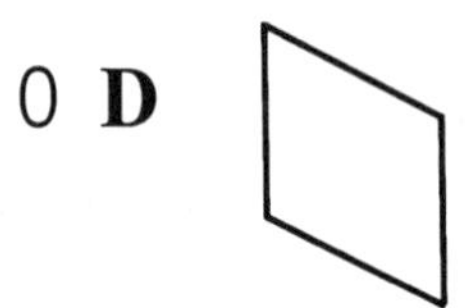

2. Which shape is NOT congruent to this one?

0 **A** 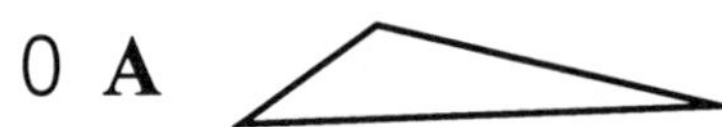

0 **B** 

0 **C** 

0 **D** 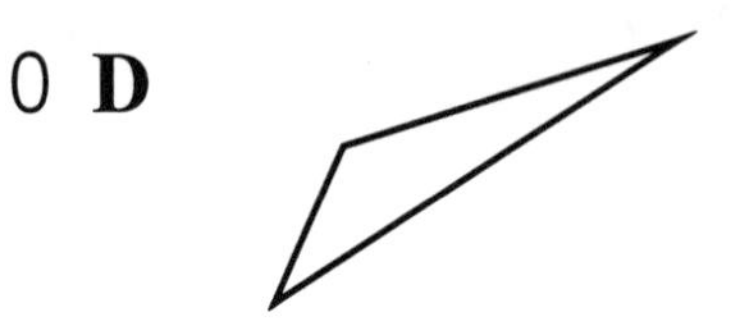

3. Which shape is congruent to this one?

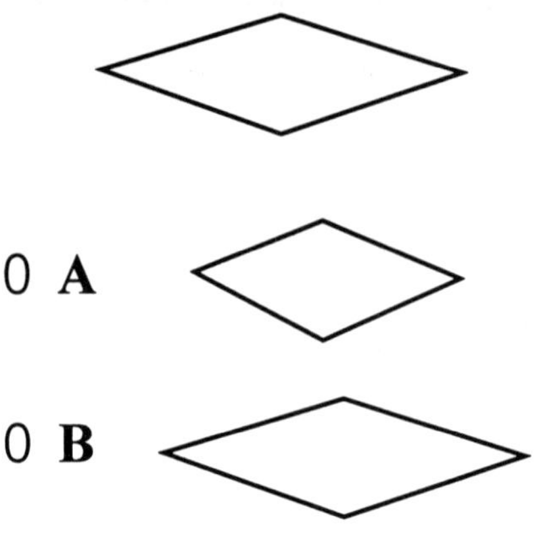

0 **A**

0 **B**

0 **C**

0 **D** 

4. Which pair of shapes is NOT congruent?

0 **A**

0 **B**

0 **C**

0 **D**

Practice 3.C1

III.C Identify lines of symmetry in shapes

1. On which shape does the dotted line show a line of symmetry?

0 **A** 

0 **B** 

0 **C** 

0 **D** 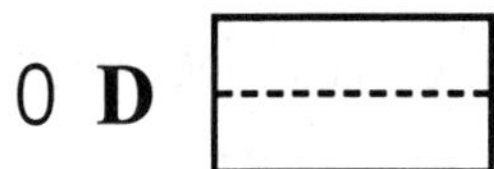

2. Which shape does NOT have at least one line of symmetry?

0 **A** 

0 **B** 

0 **C** 

0 **D** 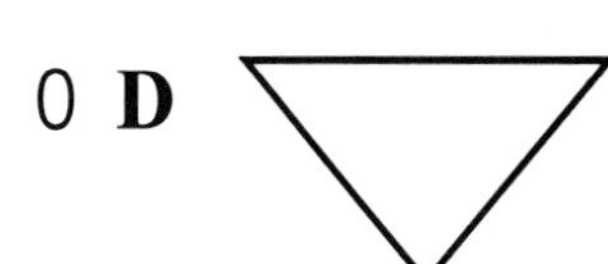

3. On which shape does the dotted line show a line of symmetry?

0 **A**

0 **B**

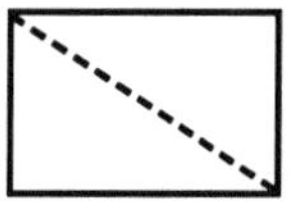

0 **C**

0 **D**

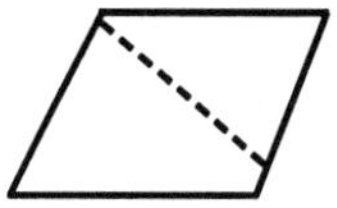

4. Which shape has at least one line of symmetry?

0 **A**

0 **B**

0 **C**

0 **D**

Practice 3.C2

III.C Identify lines of symmetry in shapes

1. Tony wants to cut the rectangle along a line of symmetry. On which line should he cut?

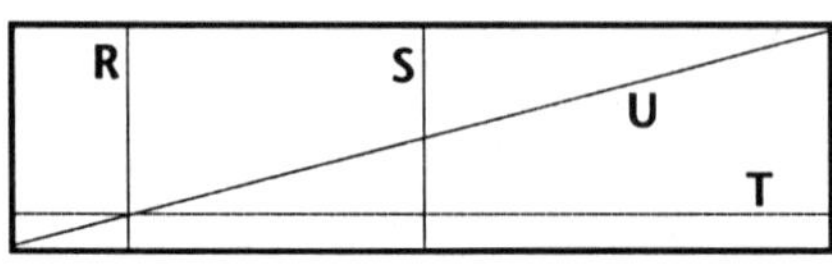

0 **A** R

0 **B** S

0 **C** T

0 **D** U

2. On which shape does the dotted line show a line of symmetry?

0 **A**

0 **B**

0 **C**

0 **D**

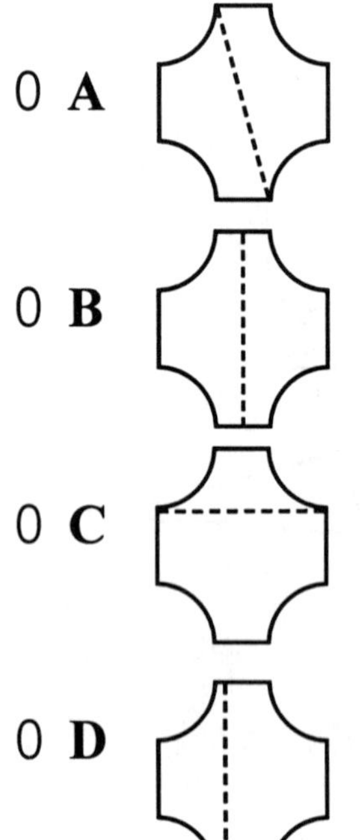

3. Which shape does NOT have at least one line of symmetry?

0 **A**

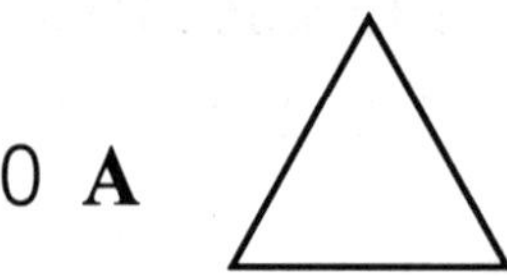

0 **B**

0 **C**

0 **D**

4. Which shape could be folded on a line of symmetry?

0 **A**

0 **B**

0 **C**

0 **D**

Practice 3.C3

III.C Identify lines of symmetry in shapes

1. Beth must cut a piece of cloth along a line of symmetry. On which line should she cut?

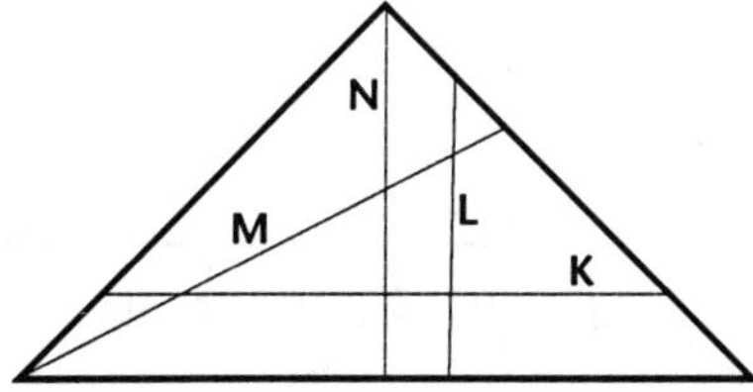

0 **A** K

0 **B** L

0 **C** M

0 **D** N

2. On which shapes does the dotted line show a line of symmetry?

0 **A** 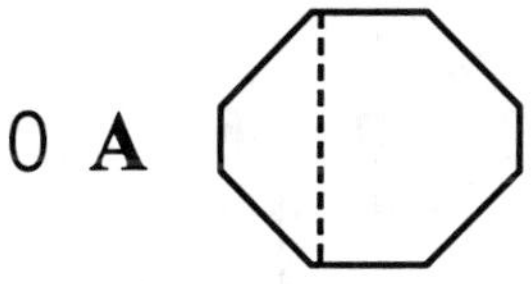

0 **B**

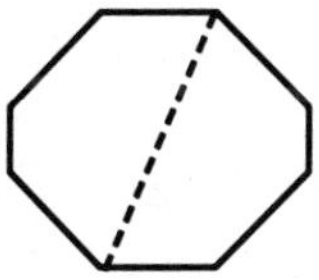

0 **C**

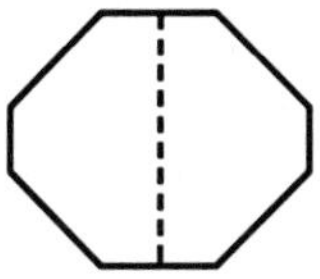

0 **D**

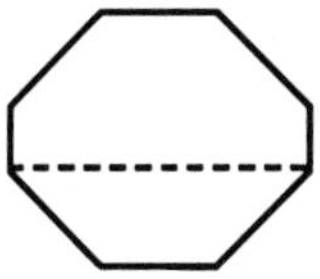

3. Which shape could be folded on a line of symmetry?

0 **A** 

0 **B** 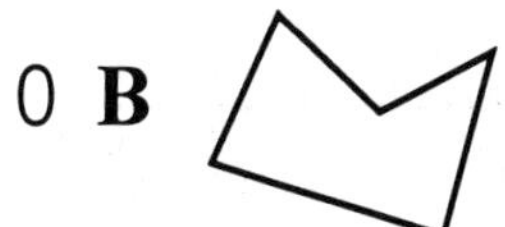

0 **C** 

0 **D** 

4. Which shape has only one line of symmetry?

0 **A**

0 **B**

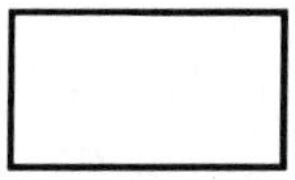

0 **C**

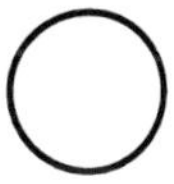

0 **D**

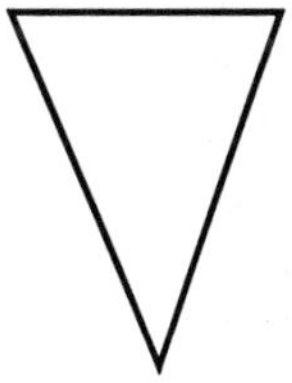

Practice 3.D1

III.D Locate and name points on a number line using whole numbers and simple fractions

1. Which number line has a star on the whole number that is between 46 and 48?

0 **A** 

0 **B** 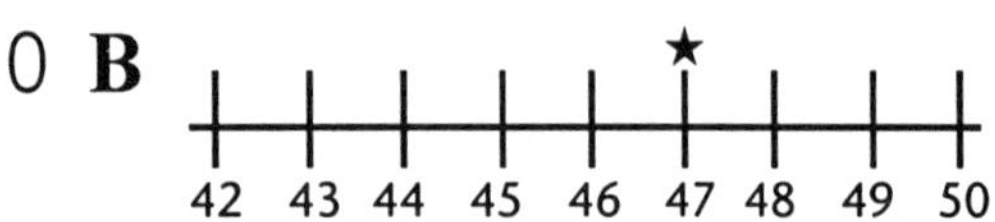

0 **C** 

0 **D** 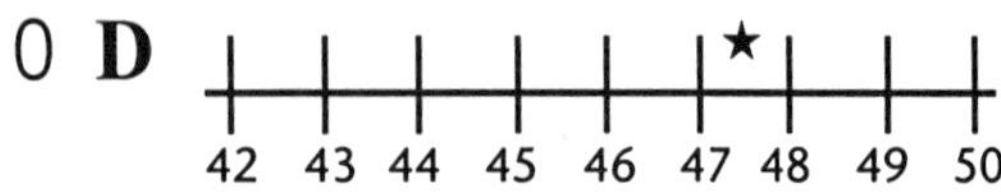

2. What number belongs where you see the letter G?

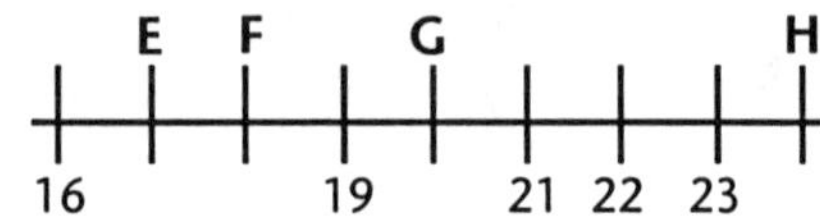

0 **A** 17

0 **B** 18

0 **C** 20

0 **D** 24

3. Which number line has a star on the whole number that is between 8 and 10?

0 **A** 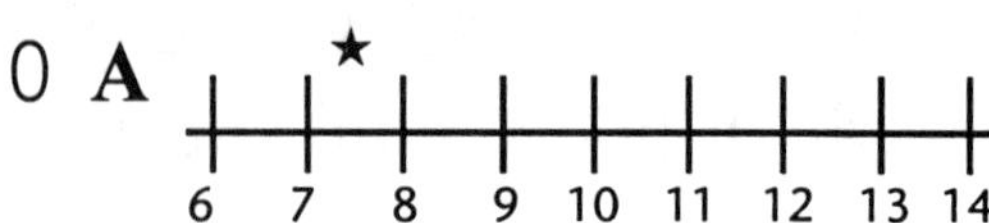

0 **B** 

0 **C** 

0 **D** 

4. What number belongs where you see the letter P?

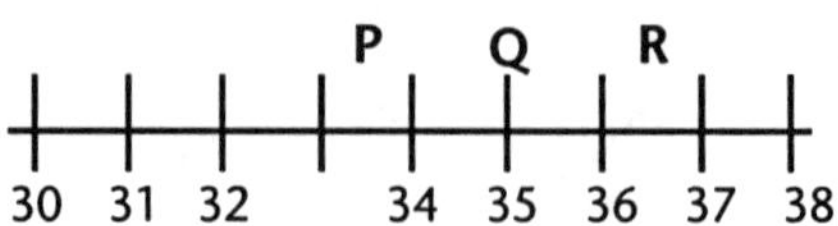

0 **A** 33

0 **B** $33\frac{1}{2}$

0 **C** 34

0 **D** $36\frac{1}{2}$

Practice 3.D2

III.D Locate and name points on a number line using whole numbers and simple fractions

1. Which number line has a star at the whole number that is between 92 and 94?

0 **A**
89 90 91 92 93 94 95 96 97

0 **B**
89 90 91 92 93 94 95 96 97

0 **C**
89 90 91 92 93 94 95 96 97

0 **D**
89 90 91 92 93 94 95 96 97

2. Which letter on the number line marks the number $18\frac{1}{2}$?

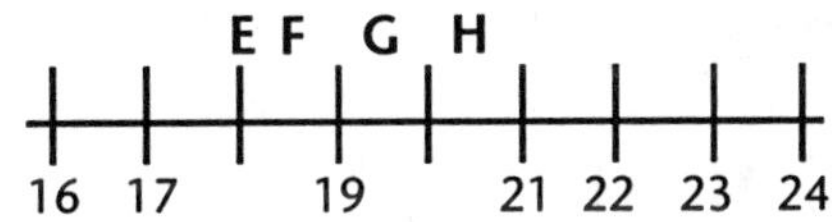

0 **A** E

0 **B** F

0 **C** G

0 **D** H

3. Which number line has a star at a whole number between 85 and 87?

0 **A**

0 **B**
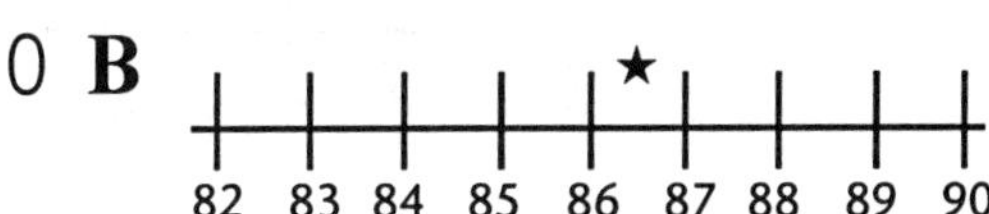

0 **C**
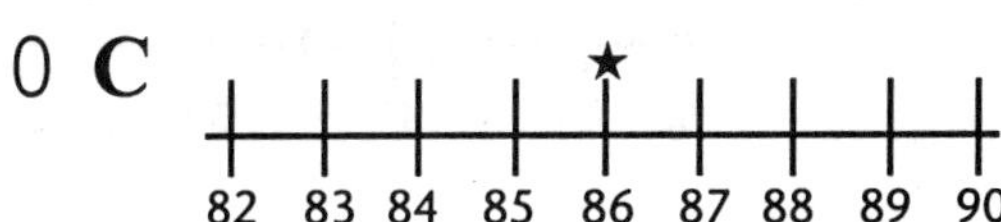

0 **D**
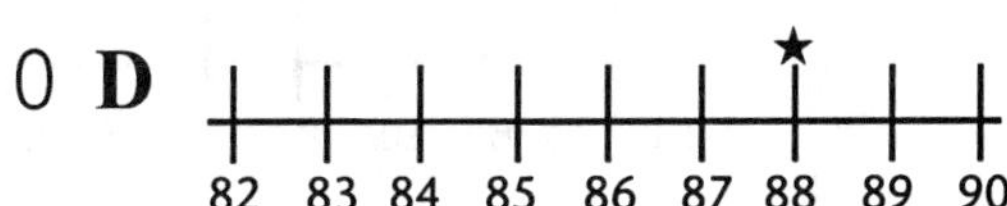

4. What number belongs where you see the letter R?

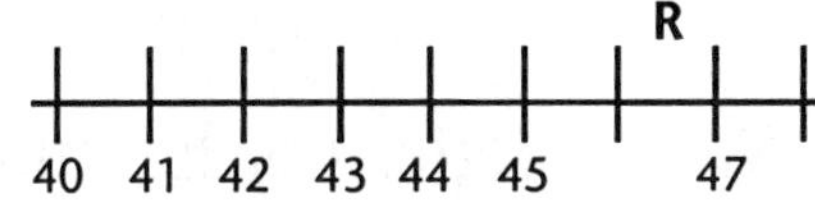

0 **A** 45

0 **B** 46

0 **C** $46\frac{1}{2}$

0 **D** 47

Practice 3.D3

III.D Locate and name points on a number line using whole numbers and simple fractions

1. Which number line has a star at a whole number that is between 84 and 87?

0 **A** 

0 **B** 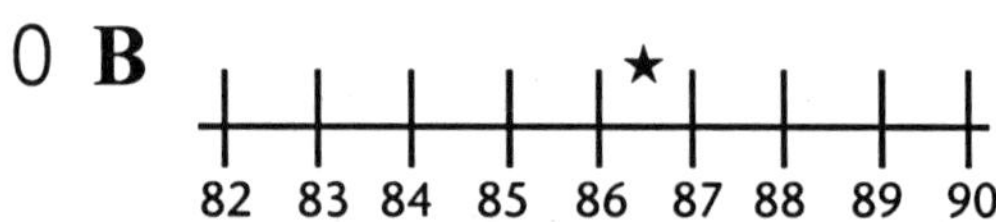

0 **C** 

0 **D** 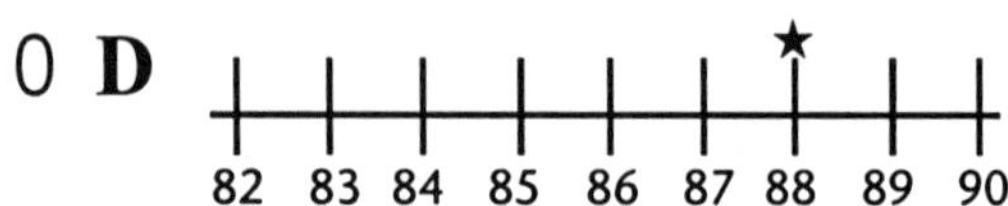

2. Which letter on the number line marks the number which is 2 more than 18?

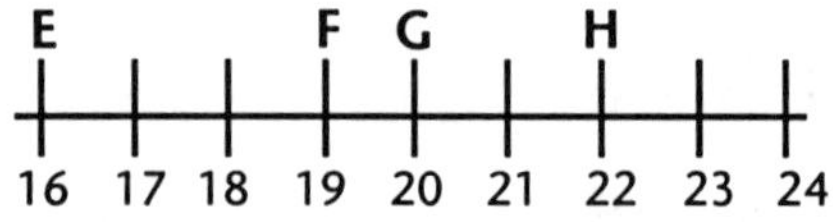

0 **A** H

0 **B** G

0 **C** F

0 **D** E

3. Which number line has a star at a whole number between 96 and 99?

0 **A** 

0 **B** 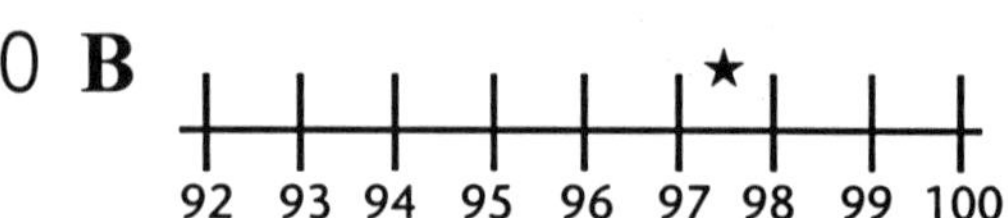

0 **C** 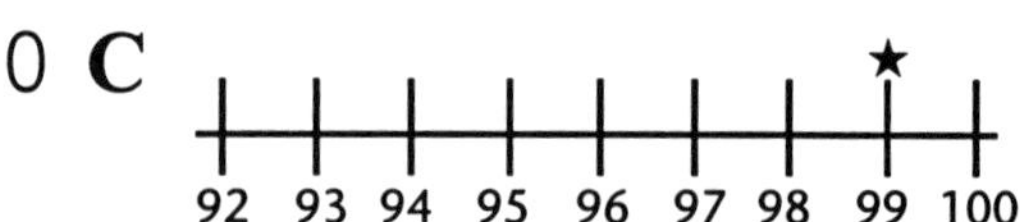

0 **D** 92 93 94 95 96 97 98 99 100

4. What number belongs where you see the letter K?

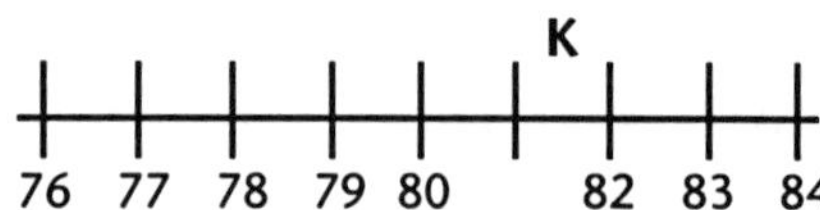

0 **A** $80\frac{1}{2}$

0 **B** 81

0 **C** $81\frac{1}{2}$

0 **D** 82

Measurement Concepts

IV. Demonstrate an understanding of measurement concepts, using metric and customary units

A. Estimate, measure, and compare lengths using standard, customary, and metric units
B. Use linear measure to find the perimeter of a shape
C. Select appropriate units for a given measurement task
D. Carry out simple unit conversions within a system of measurement
E. Estimate the area of a figure by counting squares
F. Tell and write time shown on traditional and digital clocks
G. Identify or calculate elapsed time
H. Use a thermometer to measure temperature

Notes

Objective 4: Pretest

IV.A Estimate, measure, and compare lengths using standard, customary, and metric units (1-3)

1. About how long is the line below?

0 **A** 8 inches

0 **B** 12 inches

0 **C** 2 inches

0 **D** 20 inches

2. About how long is the line below?

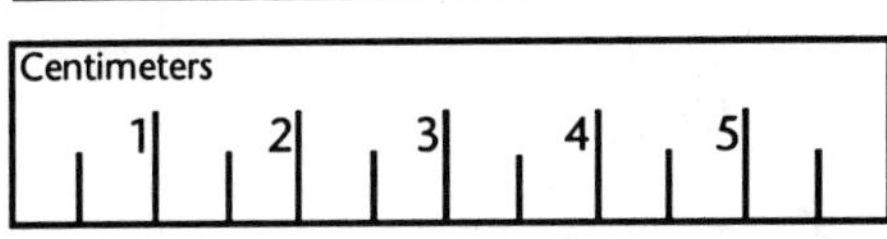

0 **A** 2 cm

0 **B** 2.5 cm

0 **C** 3 cm

0 **D** 3.5 cm

3. About how much longer is line A than line B?

A

B

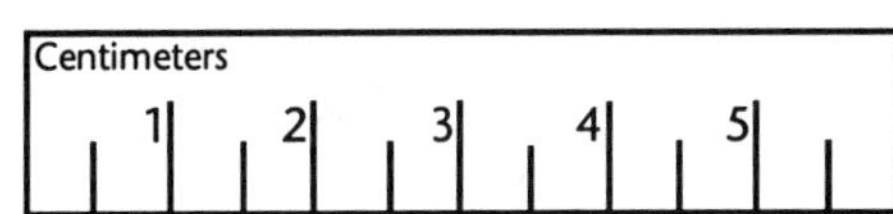

0 **A** 5.5 cm

0 **B** 3 cm

0 **C** 2 cm

0 **D** 1.5 cm

IV.B Use linear measure to find the perimeter of a shape (4-5)

4. What is the **perimeter** (distance around) the square?

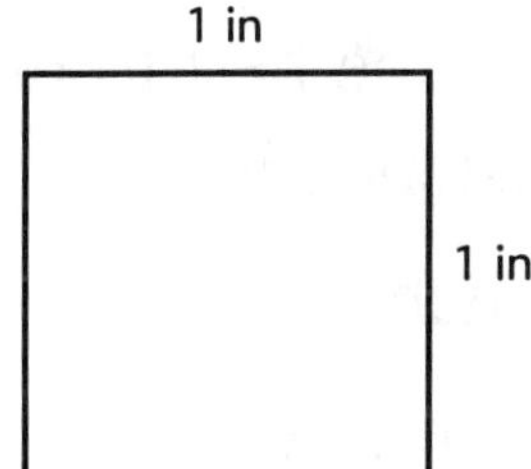

0 **A** 2 in

0 **B** 3 in

0 **C** 4 in

0 **D** 6 in

5. What is the **perimeter** (distance around) this shape?

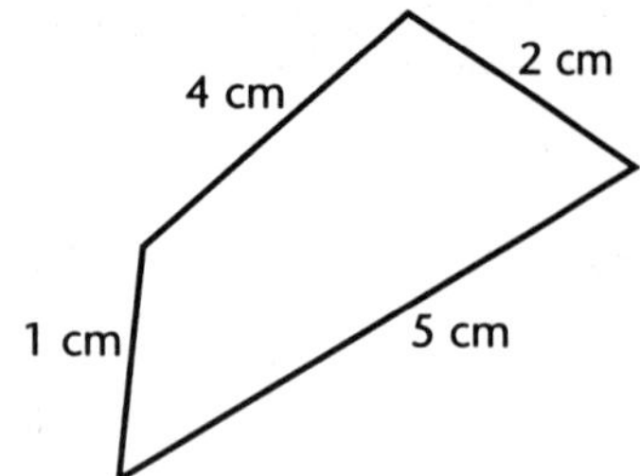

0 **A** 12 cm

0 **B** 23 cm

0 **C** 10 cm

0 **D** 14 cm

IV.C Select appropriate units for a given measurement task (6-9)

6. Missy wants to know how far she walks to school each day. It would be best to measure this distance in—

0 **A** inches

0 **B** centimeters

0 **C** feet

0 **D** miles

7. The school nurse wrote each student's weight on a chart. The nurse probably wrote each weight in—

0 **A** ounces

0 **B** pounds

0 **C** grams

0 **D** centigrams

8. Gloria used sugar to make cookies. She probably measured the sugar in—

0 **A** pints

0 **B** cups

0 **C** teaspoons

0 **D** quarts

9. Mrs. Carson bought cloth to make a dress. The cloth was probably measured in—

0 **A** inches

0 **B** centimeters

0 **C** miles

0 **D** yards

IV.D Carry out simple unit conversions within a system of measurement (10-12)

10. Mr. Mason bought 24 inches of rope. How many feet is that?

0 **A** 1 ft

0 **B** 2 ft

0 **C** 4 ft

0 **D** 6 ft

11. A package of tape holds 4 feet of tape. How many inches of tape is that?

0 **A** 16 in

0 **B** 24 in

0 **C** 36 in

0 **D** 48 in

12. Gita bought 2 meters of ribbon. How many centimeters is that?

0 **A** 20 cm

0 **B** 200 cm

0 **C** 400 cm

0 **D** 2,000 cm

IV.E Estimate the area of a figure by counting squares (13-14)

13. How many square units are in this figure?

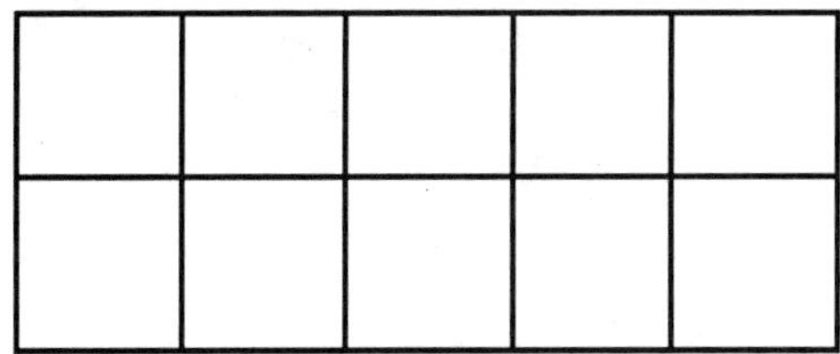

0 **A** 2

0 **B** 5

0 **C** 10

0 **D** 20

14. How many square units are shaded?

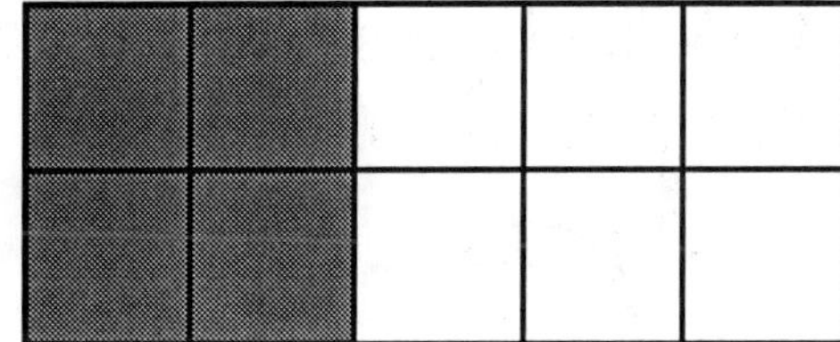

0 **A** 2

0 **B** 4

0 **C** 6

0 **D** 10

IV.F Tell and write time shown on traditional and digital clocks (15-17)

15. What time is shown on this clock?

0 **A** 3:00

0 **B** 1:25

0 **C** 2:15

0 **D** 1:15

16. Which clock shows 6:25?

0 **A** 

0 **B** 

0 **C** 

0 **D** 

17. Which clock matches the time shown below?

0 **A** 

0 **B** 

0 **C** 

0 **D** 

IV.G Identify or calculate elapsed time (18-20)

18. If it is 2:20, what time will it be 15 minutes from now?

0 **A** 2:45

0 **B** 2:40

0 **C** 2:35

0 **D** 2:25

19. Jody began watching TV 10 minutes before the time shown on the clock. What time did she begin watching TV?

0 **A** 6:10

0 **B** 5:45

0 **C** 6:00

0 **D** 5:55

20. Reading class begins at 9:15 and ends 45 minutes later. What time does reading class end?

0 **A** 10:00

0 **B** 9:55

0 **C** 9:45

0 **D** 9:40

IV.H Use a thermometer to measure temperature (21-22)

21. What temperature is shown on the thermometer?

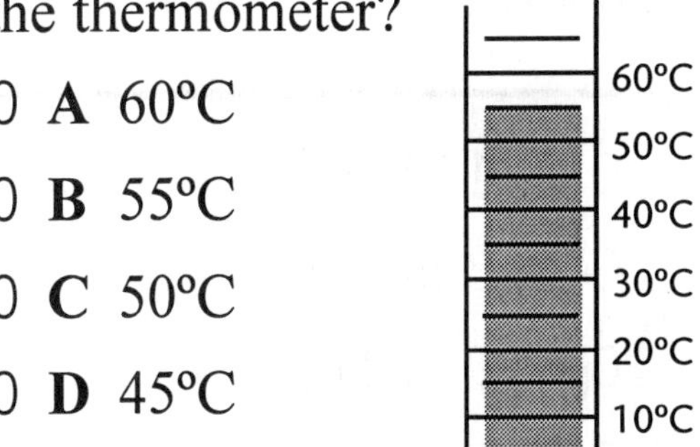

0 **A** 60°C

0 **B** 55°C

0 **C** 50°C

0 **D** 45°C

22. Which thermometer shows 45°F?

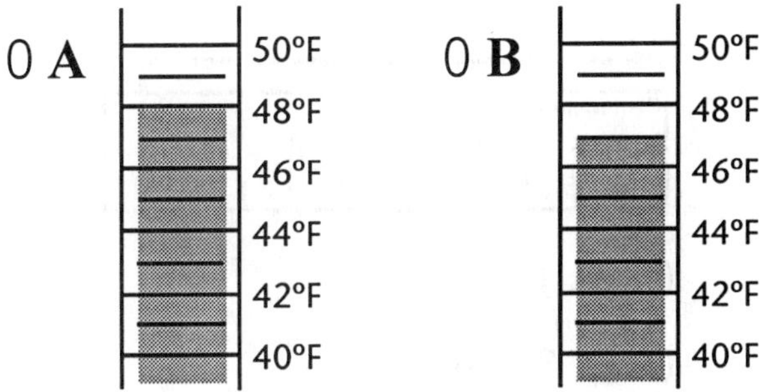

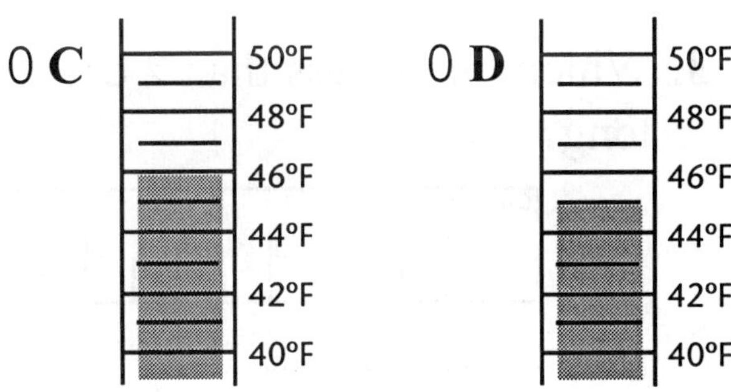

Practice 4.A1

IV.A Estimate, measure, and compare lengths using standard, customary, and metric units

1. About how long is the line below?

0 **A** 13 inches

0 **B** 3 inches

0 **C** 9 inches

0 **D** 1 inch

2. About how long is the line below?

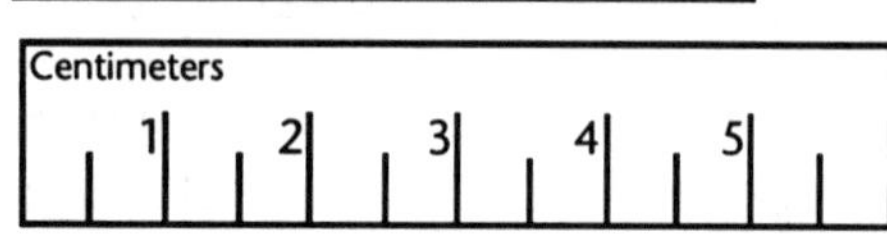

0 **A** 1 cm

0 **B** 2 cm

0 **C** 4 cm

0 **D** 5 cm

3. Which line is less than 2 cm long?

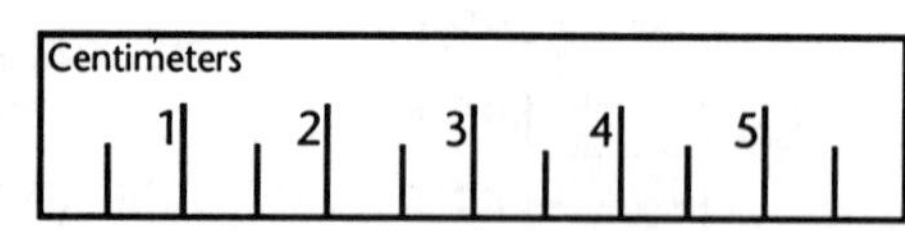

0 **A**

0 **B**

0 **C**

0 **D**

4. About how long is the line below?

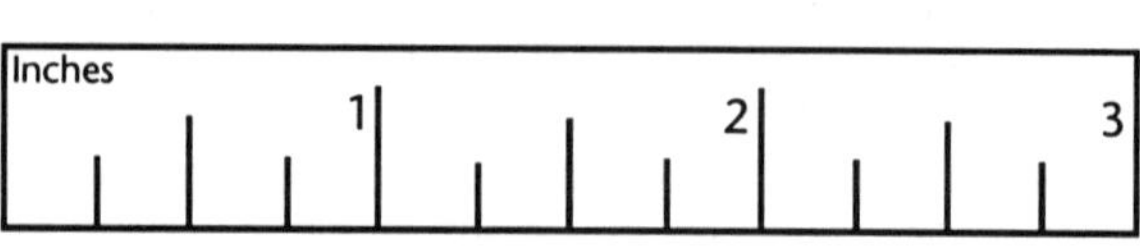

0 **A** 8 inches

0 **B** 5 inches

0 **C** 2 inches

0 **D** 1 inch

5. How much longer is line A than line B?

A

B

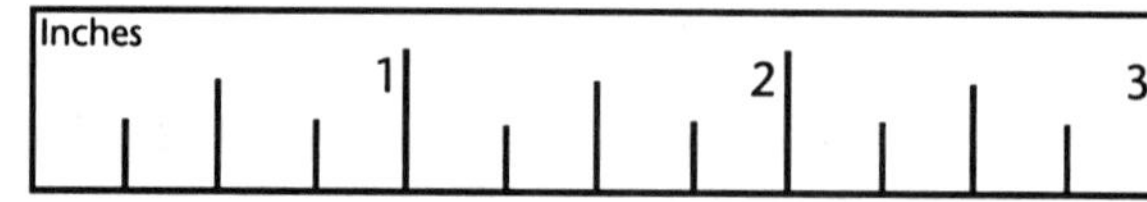

0 **A** 4 inches

0 **B** 3 inches

0 **C** 2 inches

0 **D** 1 inch

Practice 4.A2

IV.A Estimate, measure, and compare lengths using standard, customary, and metric units

1. About how long is the line below?

0 **A** 1 inch

0 **B** 3 inches

0 **C** 5 inches

0 **D** 7 inches

2. About how long is the line below?

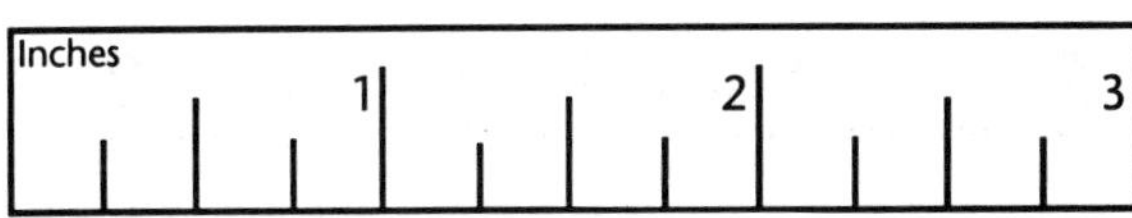

0 **A** 10 inches

0 **B** 5 inches

0 **C** $3\frac{1}{2}$ inches

0 **D** $2\frac{1}{2}$ inches

3. Which line is less than 1 inch long?

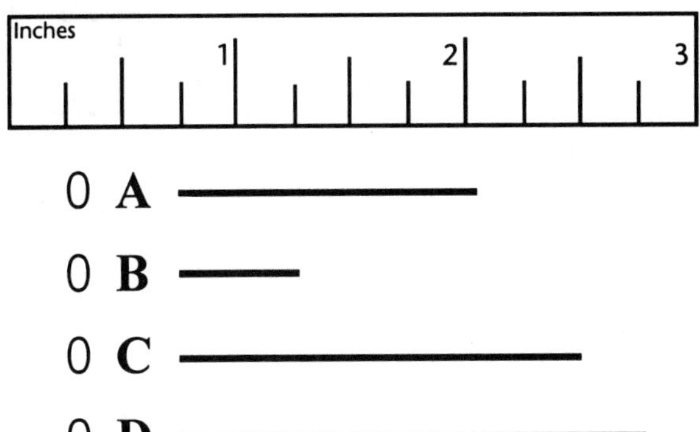

0 **A**

0 **B**

0 **C**

0 **D**

4. How much longer is line A than line B?

A

B

0 **A** 0.5 cm

0 **B** 1 cm

0 **C** 3 cm

0 **D** 4 cm

5. About how long is line A?

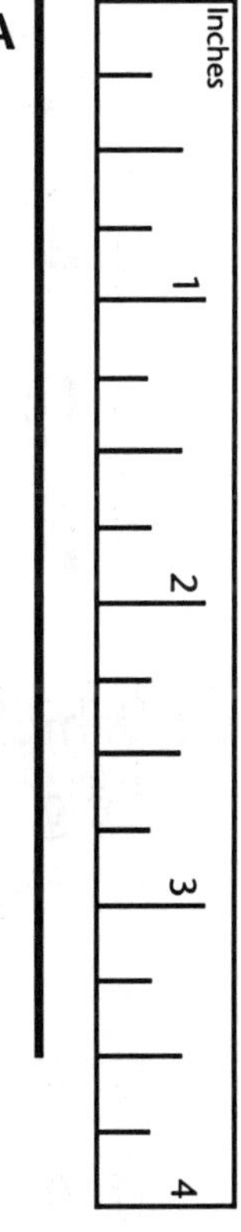

0 **A** $3\frac{1}{2}$ inches

0 **B** $4\frac{1}{2}$ inches

0 **C** 7 inches

0 **D** 14 inches

Practice 4.A3

IV.A Estimate, measure, and compare lengths using standard, customary, and metric units

1. About how long is the line below?

0 **A** 100 cm

0 **B** 50 cm

0 **C** 20 cm

0 **D** 4 cm

2. About how long is the line below?

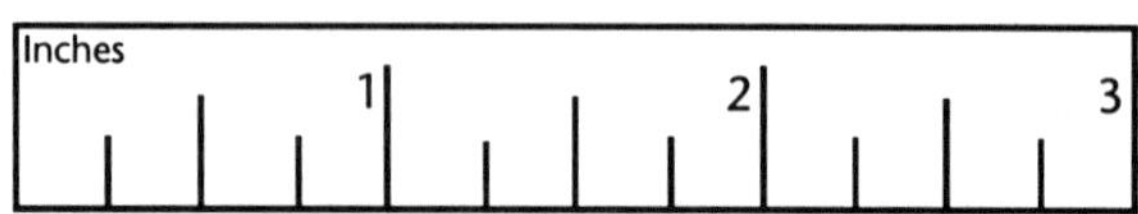

0 **A** $1\frac{1}{2}$ inches

0 **B** 2 inches

0 **C** $\frac{1}{2}$ inch

0 **D** $2\frac{1}{2}$ inches

3. Which line is more than 4 cm long?

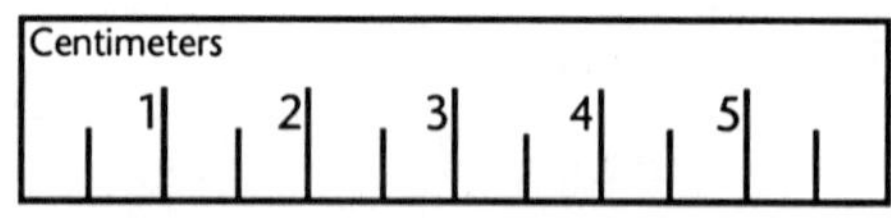

0 **A**

0 **B**

0 **C**

0 **D**

4. How much longer is line A than line B?

A

B

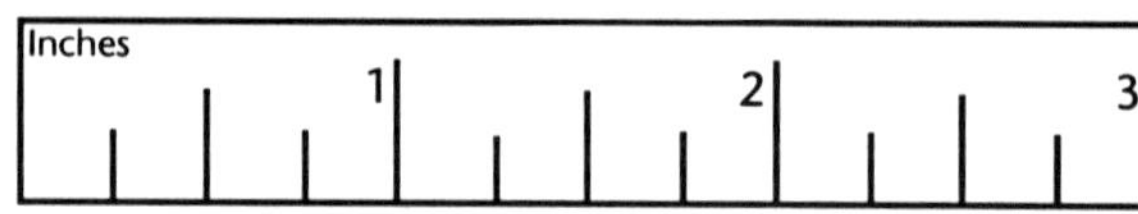

0 **A** 1 inch

0 **B** $1\frac{1}{2}$ inches

0 **C** 2 inches

0 **D** $2\frac{1}{2}$ inches

5. About how long is line A?

A

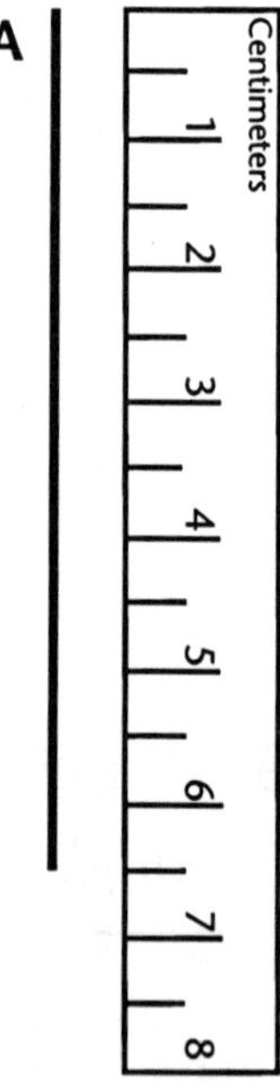

0 **A** 7 cm

0 **B** 6.5 cm

0 **C** 7.5 cm

0 **D** 6.0 cm

Practice 4.B1

IV.B Use linear measure to find the perimeter of a shape

1. What is the **perimeter** (distance around) the square?

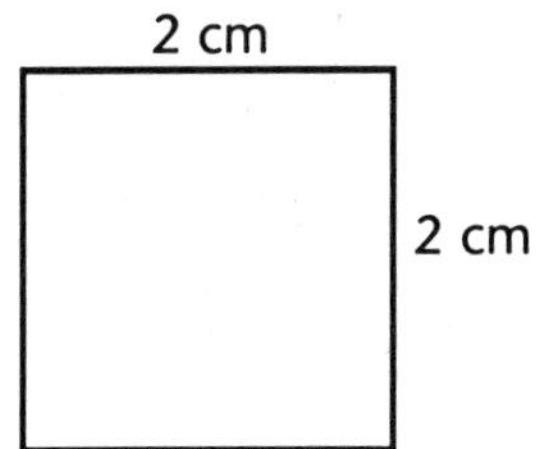

0 **A** 4 cm

0 **B** 6 cm

0 **C** 8 cm

0 **D** 10 cm

2. What is the **perimeter** (distance around) this shape?

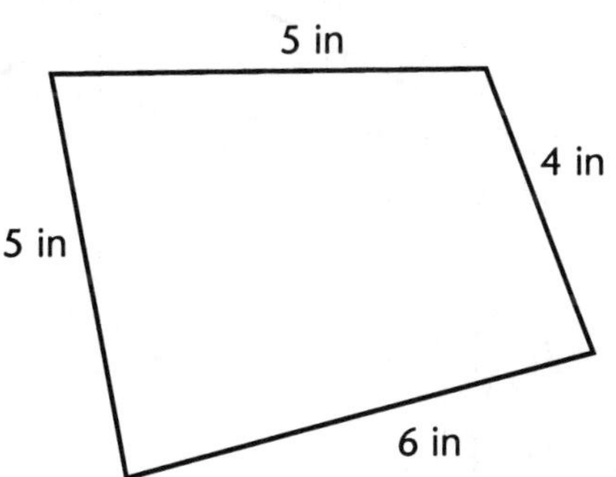

0 **A** 40 in

0 **B** 20 in

0 **C** 16 in

0 **D** 14 in

3. Dorothy walked around the playground shown below. How far did she walk?

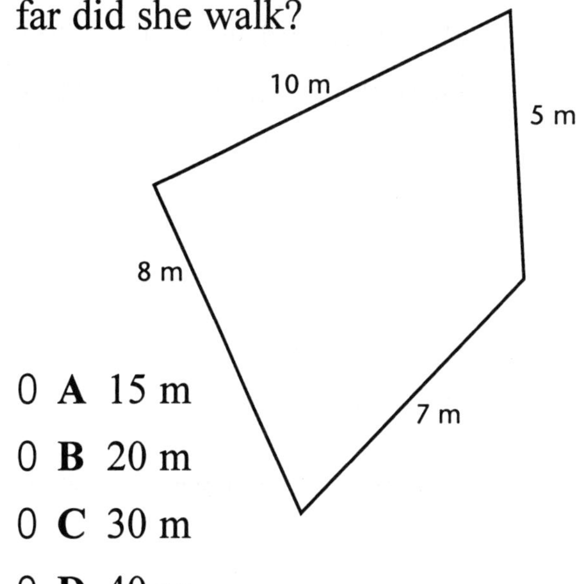

0 **A** 15 m

0 **B** 20 m

0 **C** 30 m

0 **D** 40 m

4. What is the **perimeter** (distance around) this triangle?

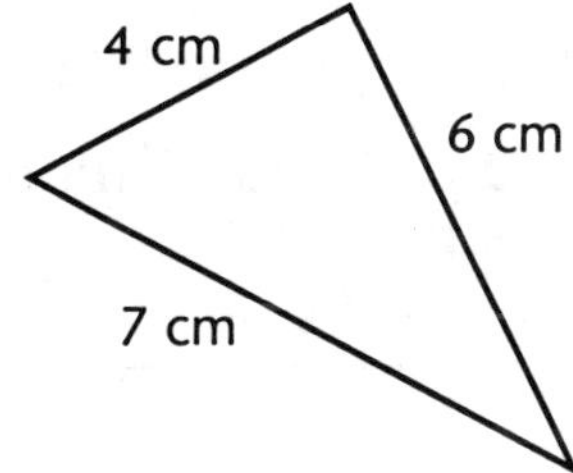

0 **A** 10 cm

0 **B** 13 cm

0 **C** 17 cm

0 **D** 31 cm

Practice 4.B2

IV.B Use linear measure to find the perimeter of a shape

1. Anna sewed lace along the **perimeter** (distance around) the tablecloth shown below. How much lace did she use?

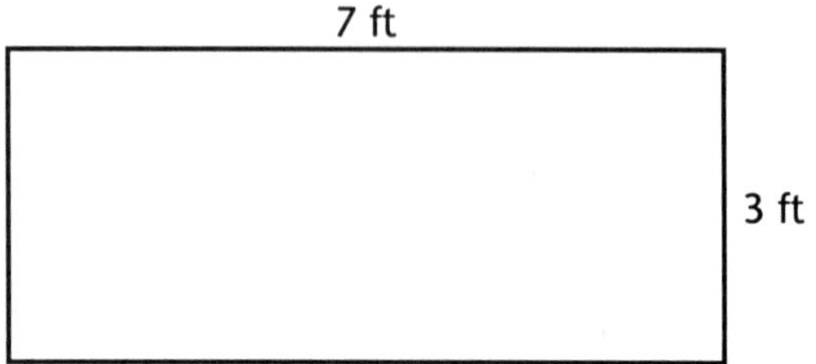

0 **A** 14 ft

0 **B** 6 ft

0 **C** 10 ft

0 **D** 20 ft

2. What is the **perimeter** (distance around) this shape?

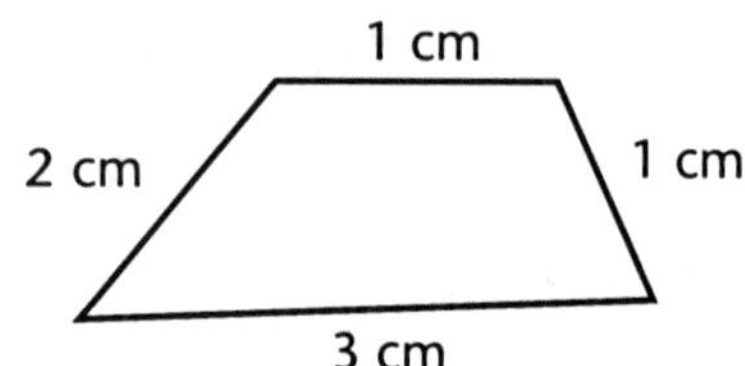

0 **A** 6 cm

0 **B** 7 cm

0 **C** 8 cm

0 **D** 10 cm

3. What is the **perimeter** (distance around) this shape?

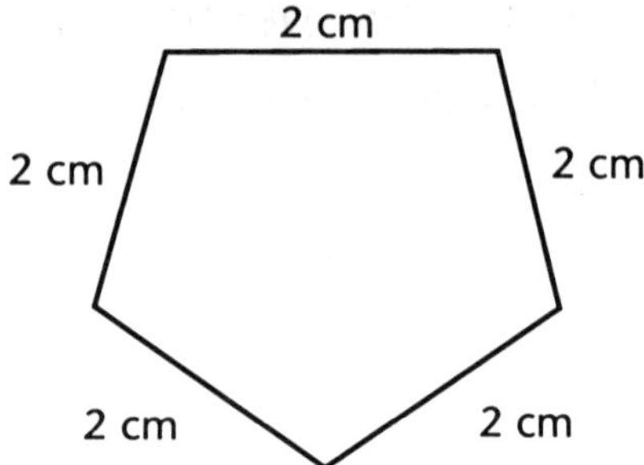

0 **A** 10 cm

0 **B** 20 cm

0 **C** 8 cm

0 **D** 16 cm

4. What is the **perimeter** (distance around) this triangle?

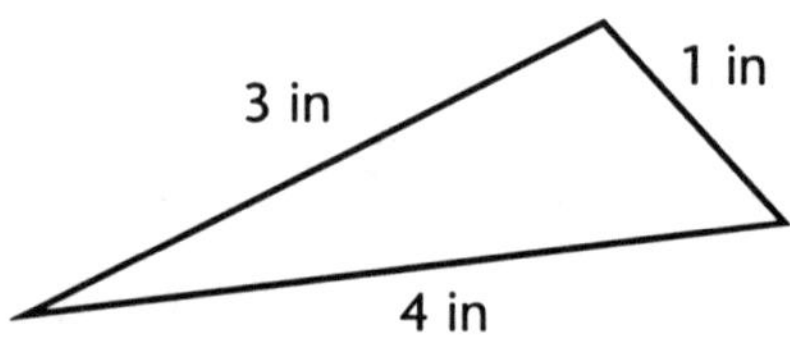

0 **A** 12 in

0 **B** 15 in

0 **C** 6 in

0 **D** 8 in

Practice 4.B3

IV.B ***Use linear measure to find the perimeter of a shape***

1. What is the **perimeter** (distance around) this rectangle?

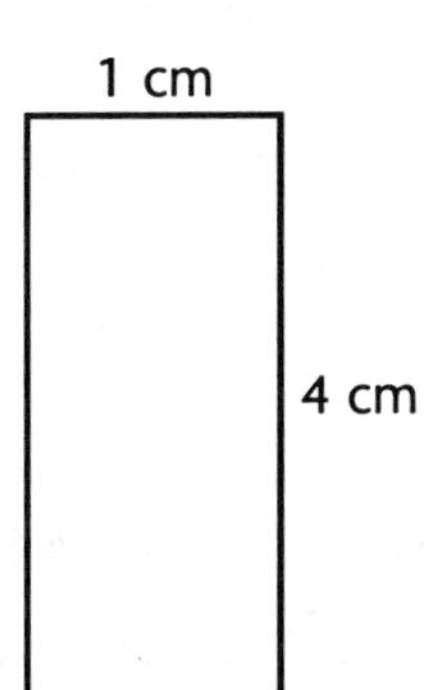

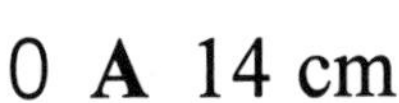

0 **A** 14 cm

0 **B** 6 cm

0 **C** 10 cm

0 **D** 20 cm

2. What is the **perimeter** (distance around) this shape?

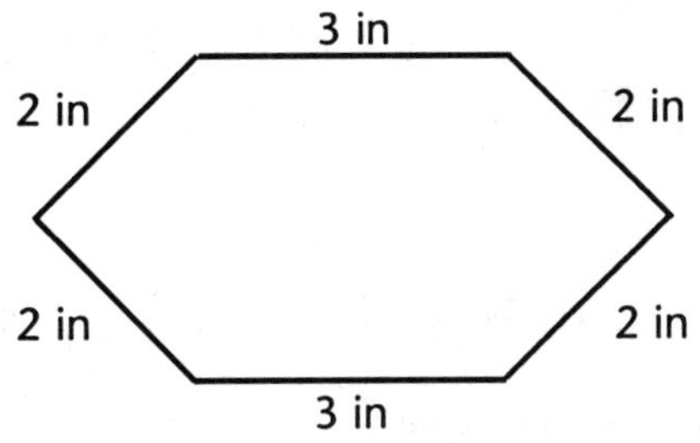

0 **A** 18 in

0 **B** 10 in

0 **C** 24 in

0 **D** 14 in

3. Eddie rode his bike around the city block shown below. How far did Eddie ride his bike?

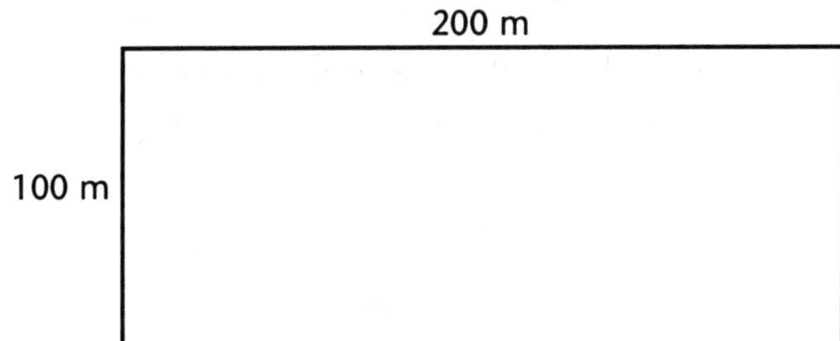

0 **A** 300 m

0 **B** 200 m

0 **C** 400 m

0 **D** 600 m

4. What is the **perimeter** (distance around) this triangle?

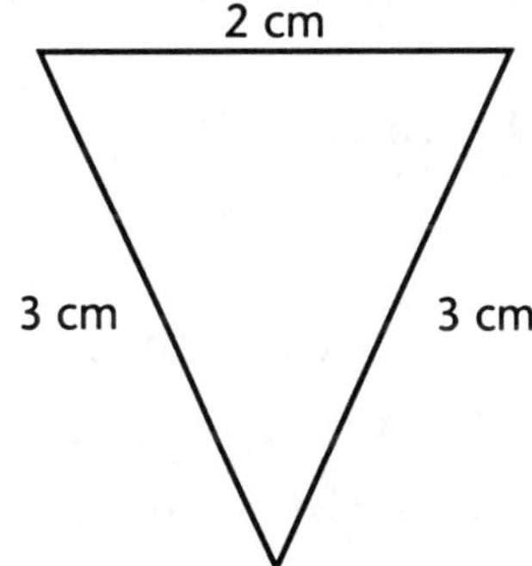

0 **A** 18 cm

0 **B** 12 cm

0 **C** 8 cm

0 **D** 6 cm

Practice 4.C1

IV.C Select appropriate units for a given measurement task

1. Mr. Craig must measure his bedroom for new carpet. He will probably measure the bedroom in square—

0 **A** inches

0 **B** centimeters

0 **C** yards

0 **D** miles

2. Mona bought apples at the store. She probably bought the apples by the—

0 **A** ounce

0 **B** pound

0 **C** cup

0 **D** gram

3. Mrs. Edgar keeps a record of how far she drives each week. She probably records this in—

0 **A** inches

0 **B** yards

0 **C** feet

0 **D** miles

4. Chuck used flour to make a cake. What amount of flour did he most likely use?

0 **A** 2 tablespoons

0 **B** 2 cups

0 **C** 2 quarts

0 **D** 2 grams

5. Spices like nutmeg and cinnamon are usually sold by the—

0 **A** pound

0 **B** kilogram

0 **C** ounce

0 **D** cup

6. About how long is your foot?

0 **A** 9 feet

0 **B** 9 inches

0 **C** 9 centimeters

0 **D** 9 yards

Practice 4.C2

IV.C Select appropriate units for a given measurement task

1. Gina added lace along the border of a tablecloth. What amount of lace did she probably use?

0 **A** 18 inches

0 **B** 18 feet

0 **C** 18 yards

0 **D** 18 centimeters

2. Kris wants to buy soil for his garden. Which is the most likely unit of measure for buying soil?

0 **A** kilogram

0 **B** gram

0 **C** milligram

0 **D** centigram

3. Kevin measured the perimeter of his back yard. What unit did he probably use?

0 **A** centimeter

0 **B** inch

0 **C** yard

0 **D** mile

4. Most people report their weight in—

0 **A** ounces

0 **B** grams

0 **C** centigrams

0 **D** pounds

5. The school nurse wrote each student's height on a chart. The nurse probably wrote each height in—

0 **A** inches

0 **B** feet and inches

0 **C** yards

0 **D** yards and feet

6. Eliza bought cloth to make a vest. The cloth was probably measured in—

0 **A** inches

0 **B** centimeters

0 **C** yards

0 **D** miles

Practice 4.C3

IV.C Select appropriate units for a given measurement task

1. Which unit is best to measure the weight of a pencil?

0 **A** pound

0 **B** yard

0 **C** gram

0 **D** inch

2. Toby wants to measure the length of the classroom. Which unit of measure should he use?

0 **A** inch

0 **B** yard

0 **C** centimeter

0 **D** pound

3. Anna buys string to make necklaces for her friends. Which unit would be best for buying string?

0 **A** foot

0 **B** centimeter

0 **C** gram

0 **D** kilogram

4. What unit is best to measure how much water a drinking glass will hold?

0 **A** quart

0 **B** pint

0 **C** ounce

0 **D** pound

5. Kenny stood at one end of the sidewalk and jumped as far as he could. Which unit would be best to measure how far Kenny jumped?

0 **A** mile

0 **B** centimeter

0 **C** inch

0 **D** foot

6. Which unit is best to measure the weight of a packed suitcase?

0 **A** kilogram

0 **B** gram

0 **C** ounce

0 **D** cup

Practice 4.D1

IV.D Carry out simple unit conversions within a system of measurement

1. A bag holds 2 pounds of candy. How many ounces is that?

0 **A** 20 oz

0 **B** 16 oz

0 **C** 32 oz

0 **D** 8 oz

2. Dana used 24 inches of lace on her jacket. How many feet is that?

0 **A** 2 ft

0 **B** 4 ft

0 **C** 6 ft

0 **D** 8 ft

3. Jacob bought 250 centimeters of rope. How many meters is that?

0 **A** 20 m

0 **B** 2 m

0 **C** 4 m

0 **D** 2.5 m

4. Suzanne drank 2 pints of milk. How many cups is that?

0 **A** 8 cups

0 **B** 6 cups

0 **C** 4 cups

0 **D** 2 cups

5. A can holds 4 cups of juice. How many ounces is that?

0 **A** 16 oz

0 **B** 24 oz

0 **C** 28 oz

0 **D** 32 oz

6. Tori bought 2 yards of ribbon. How many feet is that?

0 **A** 4 ft

0 **B** 6 ft

0 **C** 10 ft

0 **D** 24 ft

Practice 4.D2

IV.D Carry out simple unit conversions within a system of measurement

1. Billy used 4 feet of ribbon on a package. How many inches is that?

0 **A** 10 in

0 **B** 24 in

0 **C** 40 in

0 **D** 48 in

2. A jar holds 3,000 grams of water. How many kilograms is that?

0 **A** 10 kg

0 **B** 5 kg

0 **C** 3 kg

0 **D** 1 kg

3. The **perimeter** (distance around) a room is 36 feet. How many yards is that?

0 **A** 3 yd

0 **B** 4 yd

0 **C** 8 yd

0 **D** 12 yd

4. A pitcher holds 8 cups of lemonade. How many pints is that?

0 **A** 1 pint

0 **B** 2 pints

0 **C** 4 pints

0 **D** 8 pints

5. A jug holds 8 quarts of water. How many gallons is that?

0 **A** 1 gallon

0 **B** 2 gallons

0 **C** 4 gallons

0 **D** 8 gallons

6. The distance around a track is 5,000 meters. How many kilometers is that?

0 **A** 1 km

0 **B** 2 km

0 **C** 5 km

0 **D** 10 km

Practice 4.D3

IV.D Carry out simple unit conversions within a system of measurement

1. A bag of candy weighs 3 pounds. How many ounces is that?

0 **A** 3 oz

0 **B** 30 oz

0 **C** 36 oz

0 **D** 48 oz

2. A library table is 450 centimeters long. How many meters is that?

0 **A** 3 m

0 **B** 4 m

0 **C** 4.5 m

0 **D** 5 m

3. Uma hiked 3.5 kilometers. How many meters is that?

0 **A** 3,500 m

0 **B** 350 m

0 **C** 305 m

0 **D** 35 m

4. The **perimeter** (distance around) a rectangle is 1 foot. How many inches is that?

0 **A** 8 in

0 **B** 10 in

0 **C** 12 in

0 **D** 18 in

5. A bucket holds 8 gallons of water. How many quarts is that?

0 **A** 16 quarts

0 **B** 32 quarts

0 **C** 36 quarts

0 **D** 48 quarts

6. A football player ran 6 yards for a touchdown. How many feet is that?

0 **A** 18 ft

0 **B** 20 ft

0 **C** 24 ft

0 **D** 36 ft

Practice 4.E1

IV.E Estimate the area of a figure by counting squares

1. How many square units are in this figure?

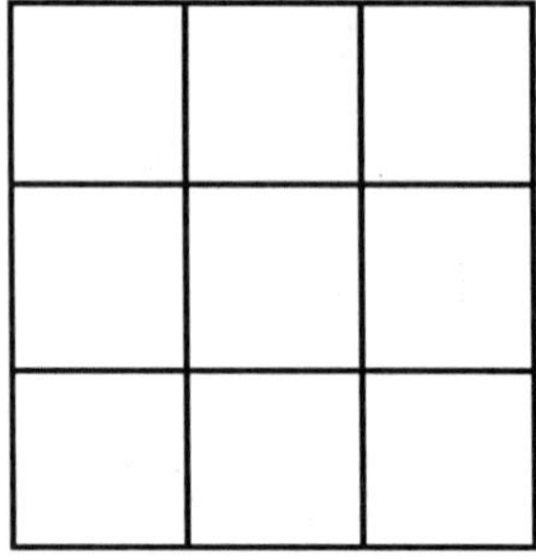

0 **A** 6

0 **B** 8

0 **C** 9

0 **D** 12

2. How many square units are shaded?

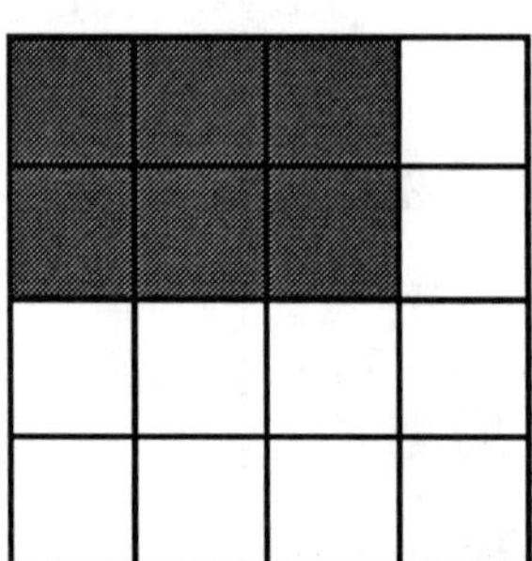

0 **A** 3

0 **B** 6

0 **C** 8

0 **D** 10

3. Look at the triangle inside the square.

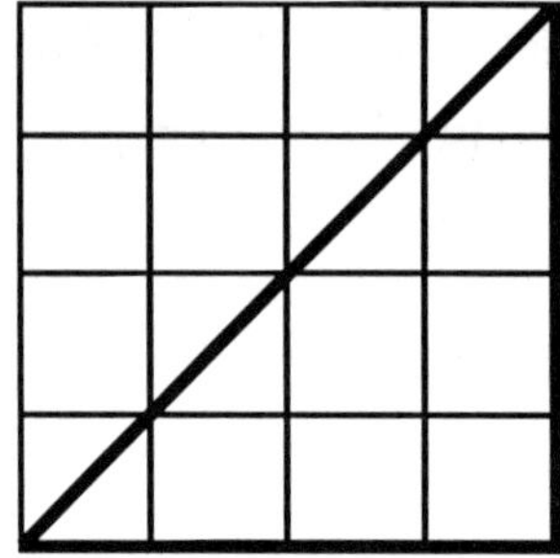

The **area** of the triangle is about—

0 **A** 8 square units

0 **B** 6 square units

0 **C** 4 square units

0 **D** 2 square units

4. What is the **area** of this rectangle?

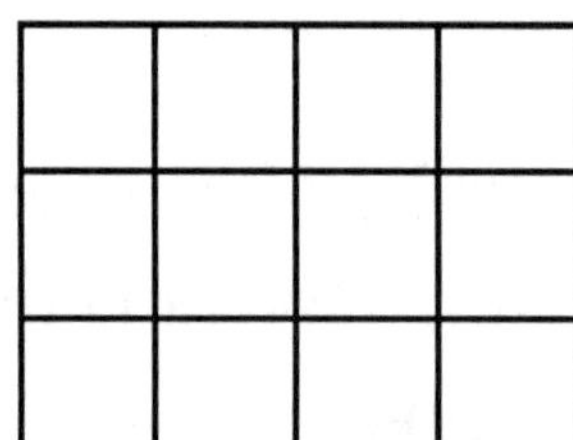

0 **A** 6 square units

0 **B** 8 square units

0 **C** 10 square units

0 **D** 12 square units

Practice 4.E2

IV.E Estimate the area of a figure by counting squares

1. How many square units are in this figure?

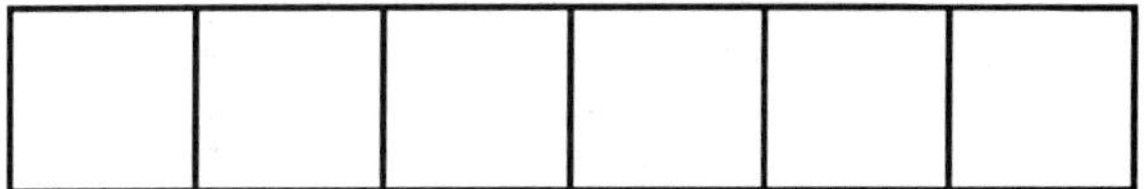

0 **A** 7

0 **B** 6

0 **C** 5

0 **D** 4

2. Look at the shaded part of the rectangle.

The **area** of the shaded part is about—

0 **A** 10 square units

0 **B** 8 square units

0 **C** 5 square units

0 **D** 4 square units

3. Look at the rectangle inside the square.

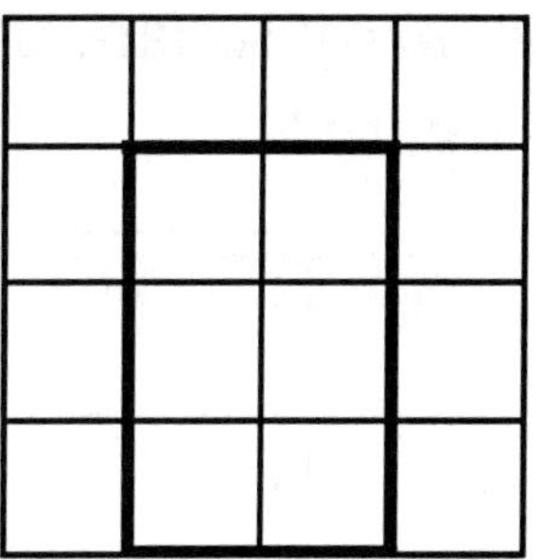

The **area** of the rectangle is about—

0 **A** 16 square units

0 **B** 10 square units

0 **C** 6 square units

0 **D** 4 square units

4. What is the **area** of this shape?

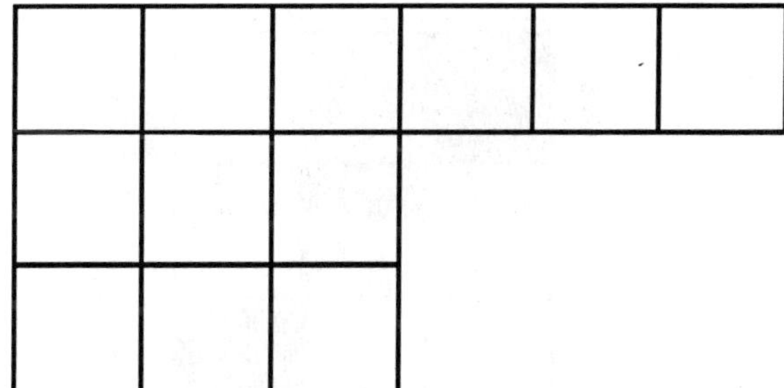

0 **A** 3 square units

0 **B** 6 square units

0 **C** 9 square units

0 **D** 12 square units

Practice 4.E3

IV.E Estimate the area of a figure by counting squares

1. How many square units are in this figure?

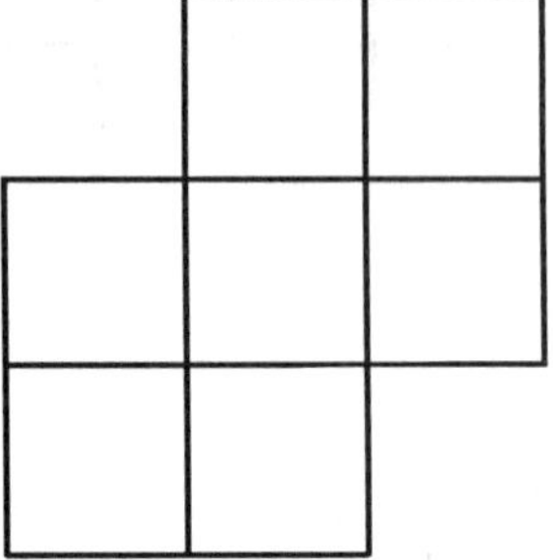

0 **A** 7

0 **B** 6

0 **C** 5

0 **D** 4

2. Look at the shaded part of the square.

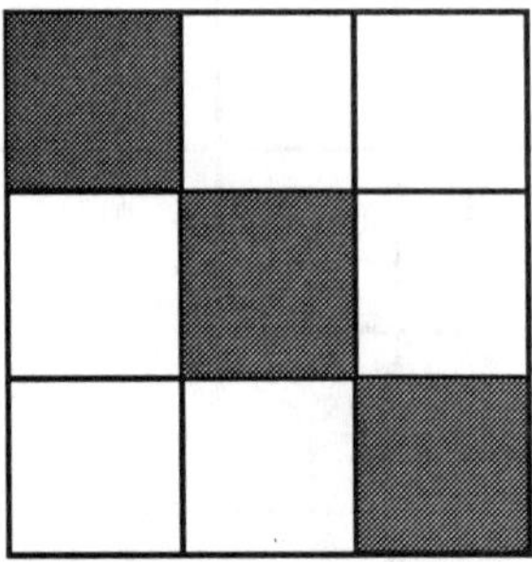

The **area** of the shaded part is—

0 **A** 9 square units

0 **B** 8 square units

0 **C** 6 square units

0 **D** 3 square units

3. Look at the shaded part of the shape.

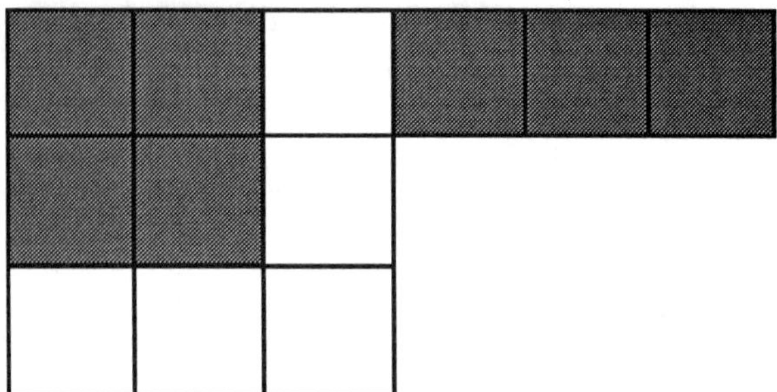

The **area** of the shaded part is—

0 **A** 5 square units

0 **B** 7 square units

0 **C** 9 square units

0 **D** 12 square units

4. What is the **area** of this shape?

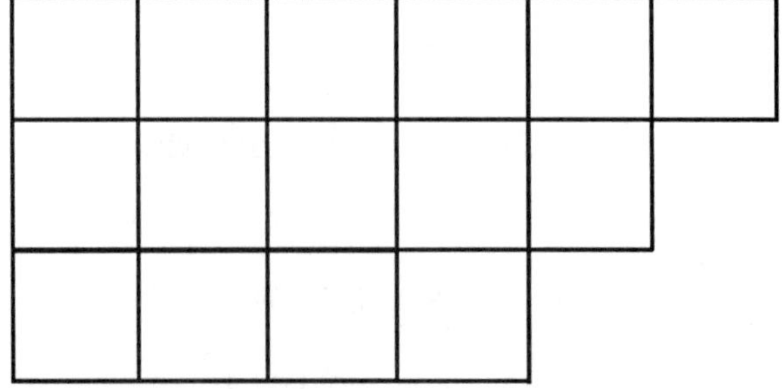

0 **A** 9 square units

0 **B** 12 square units

0 **C** 15 square units

0 **D** 18 square units

Practice 4.F1

IV.F Tell and write time shown on traditional and digital clocks

1. What time is shown on this clock?

0 **A** 1:30

0 **B** 2:15

0 **C** 2:30

0 **D** 3:30

2. Which clock shows 7:20?

0 **A** 

0 **B** 

0 **C** 

0 **D** 

3. Which clock matches the time shown below?

0 **A** 

0 **B** 

0 **C** 

0 **D** 

4. What time is shown on this clock?

0 **A** 6:20

0 **B** 4:30

0 **C** 4:20

0 **D** 3:30

Practice 4.F2

IV.F Tell and write time shown on traditional and digital clocks

1. What time is shown on this clock?

0 **A** 1:20

0 **B** 1:25

0 **C** 2:25

0 **D** 2:30

2. Which clock shows 9:05?

0 **A** 

0 **B** 

0 **C** 

0 **D** 

3. Which clock matches the time shown below?

0 **A** 

0 **B** 

0 **C** 

0 **D** 

4. What time is shown on this clock?

0 **A** 6:40

0 **B** 6:30

0 **C** 6:20

0 **D** 6:10

Practice 4.F3

***IV.F** Tell and write time shown on traditional and digital clocks*

1. What time is shown on this clock?

0 **A** 3:05
0 **B** 3:10
0 **C** 3:15
0 **D** 3:25

2. Which clock shows 10:25?

0 **A** 

0 **B** 

0 **C** 

0 **D** 

3. Which clock matches the time shown below?

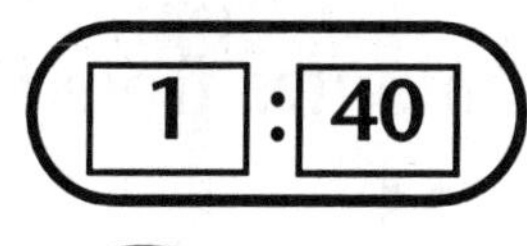

0 **A** 

0 **B** 

0 **C** 

0 **D** 

4. What time is shown on this clock?

0 **A** 1:30
0 **B** 7:00
0 **C** 7:05
0 **D** 7:55

Practice 4.G1

IV.G Identify or calculate elapsed time

1. If it is 1:15, what time will it be 15 minutes from now?

0 **A** 1:25

0 **B** 1:30

0 **C** 1:45

0 **D** 2:00

2. Glenn woke up at 4:30. He had been asleep for 25 minutes. What time did he fall asleep?

0 **A** 4:55

0 **B** 4:45

0 **C** 4:15

0 **D** 4:05

3. Mrs. Minton left her house for work at 2:15. She drove for 25 minutes. What time did she get to work?

0 **A** 2:50

0 **B** 2:45

0 **C** 2:40

0 **D** 2:30

4. Annie began reading 15 minutes before the time shown on the clock. What time did she begin reading?

0 **A** 2:05

0 **B** 2:15

0 **C** 2:25

0 **D** 2:45

5. Mr. Angelo spent 50 minutes cooking dinner. He began at 5:20. What time did he finish?

0 **A** 5:25

0 **B** 5:55

0 **C** 6:05

0 **D** 6:10

Practice 4.G2

IV.G Identify or calculate elapsed time

1. Jenny listened to her favorite CD for 35 minutes. She quit listening at 4:25. What time did she begin?

0 **A** 4:00

0 **B** 3:50

0 **C** 3:45

0 **D** 3:25

2. Danny hiked for 40 minutes. He began hiking at 2:15. What time did he finish?

0 **A** 2:55

0 **B** 2:45

0 **C** 2:35

0 **D** 2:25

3. Mrs. Tanner began her exercises at 6:15. She finished 30 minutes later. What time did she finish?

0 **A** 6:30

0 **B** 6:35

0 **C** 6:45

0 **D** 6:50

4. A bus driver left the bus barn at the time shown on the clock and drove 20 minutes to the school. What time did he get to the school?

0 **A** 7:25

0 **B** 7:30

0 **C** 7:40

0 **D** 7:50

5. Mr. Peterson began reading at 6:30. He read for 55 minutes. What time did he stop reading?

0 **A** 7:35

0 **B** 7:25

0 **C** 7:15

0 **D** 6:55

Practice 4.G3

IV.G Identify or calculate elapsed time

1. A TV show began at 5:05 and ended 35 minutes later. What time did the show end?

0 **A** 5:25

0 **B** 5:30

0 **C** 5:35

0 **D** 5:40

2. Dylan must practice playing the piano 45 minutes every day. If he begins practice at 6:30, when can he stop?

0 **A** 7:15

0 **B** 7:10

0 **C** 6:55

0 **D** 6:45

3. A batch of cookies must bake for 20 minutes. If Janice puts a batch of cookies in the oven at 3:25, when will they be finished?

0 **A** 3:35

0 **B** 3:40

0 **C** 3:45

0 **D** 3:55

4. Carol left home at the time shown on the clock and walked for 35 minutes. What time did she stop walking?

0 **A** 9:40

0 **B** 9:45

0 **C** 9:50

0 **D** 9:55

5. Mr. Chacko swims for 45 minutes each day. If he begins swimming at 5:10, when will he stop?

0 **A** 6:00

0 **B** 5:55

0 **C** 5:50

0 **D** 5:35

Practice 4.H1

IV.H Use a thermometer to measure temperature

1. What temperature is shown on the thermometer?

0 **A** 41°F

0 **B** 40°F

0 **C** 39°F

0 **D** 38°F

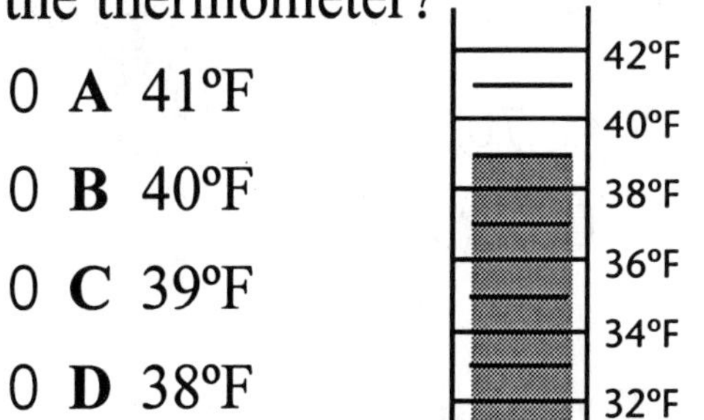

2. Which thermometer shows 55°C?

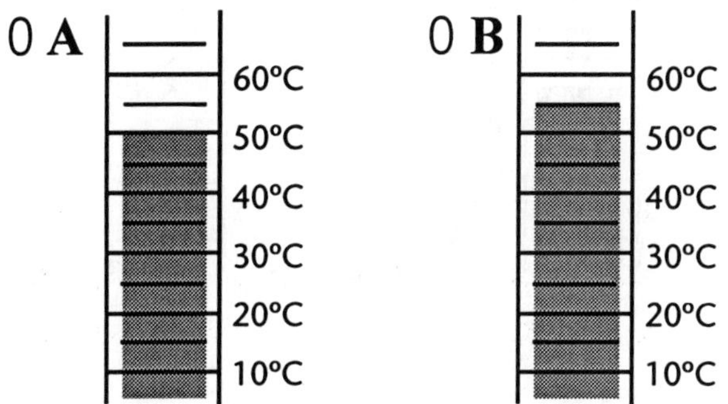

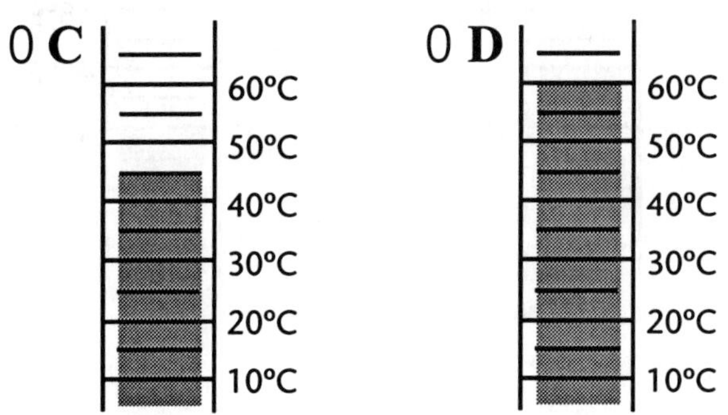

3. What temperature is shown on the thermometer?

0 **A** 35°C

0 **B** 30°C

0 **C** 28°C

0 **D** 25°C

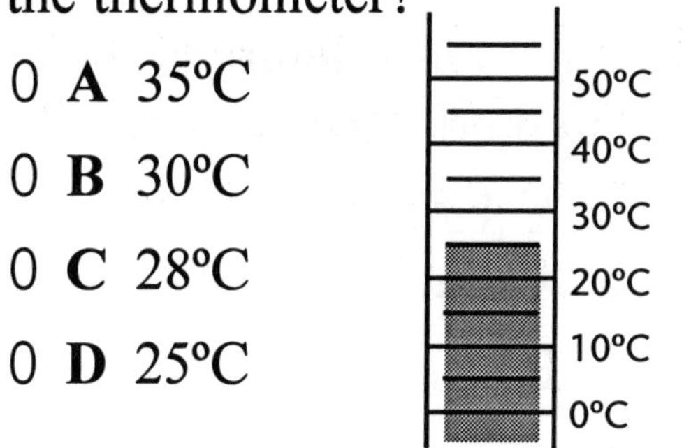

4. Which thermometer shows 57°F?

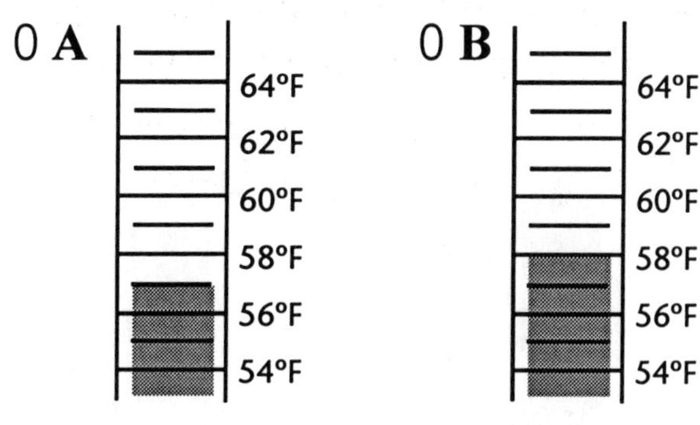

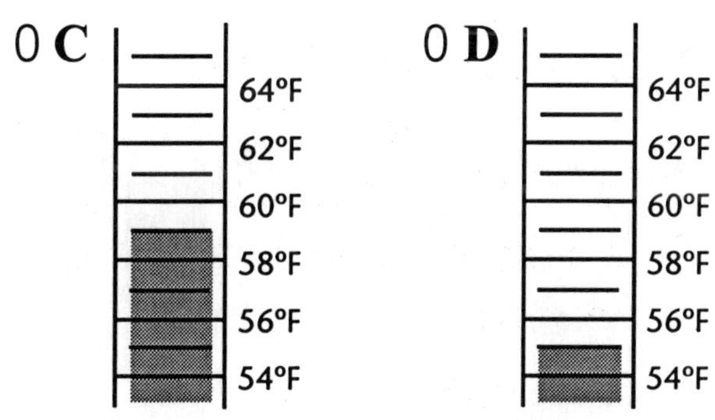

Practice 4.H2

IV.H Use a thermometer to measure temperature

1. What temperature is shown on the thermometer?

0 **A** 75°F

0 **B** 74°F

0 **C** 73°F

0 **D** 70°F

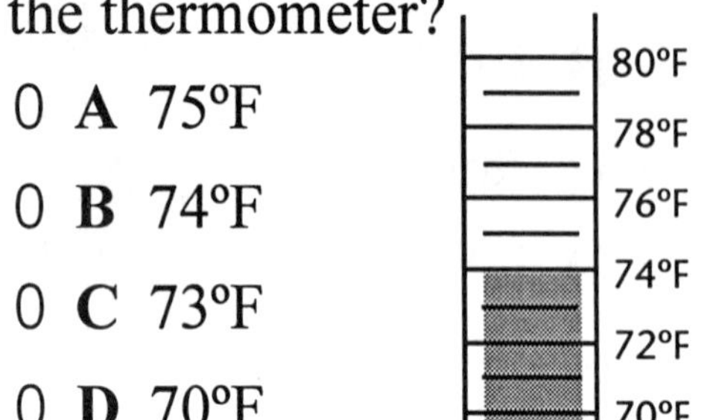

2. Which thermometer shows 25°C?

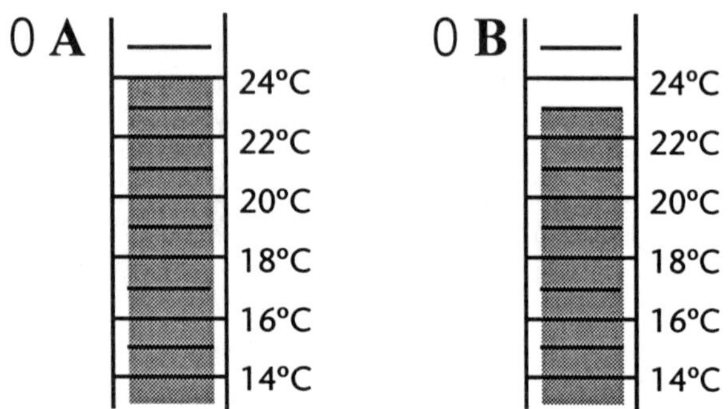

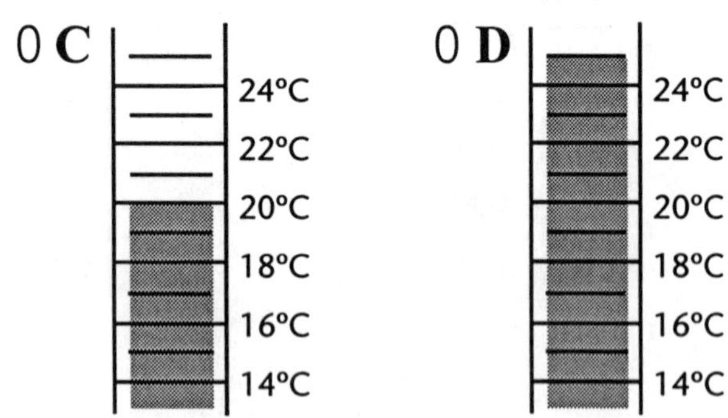

3. What temperature is shown on the thermometer?

0 **A** 60°C

0 **B** 65°C

0 **C** 70°C

0 **D** 75°C

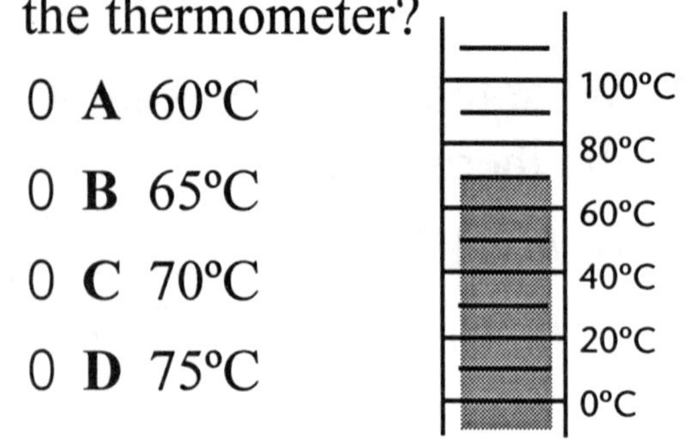

4. Which thermometer shows 42°F?

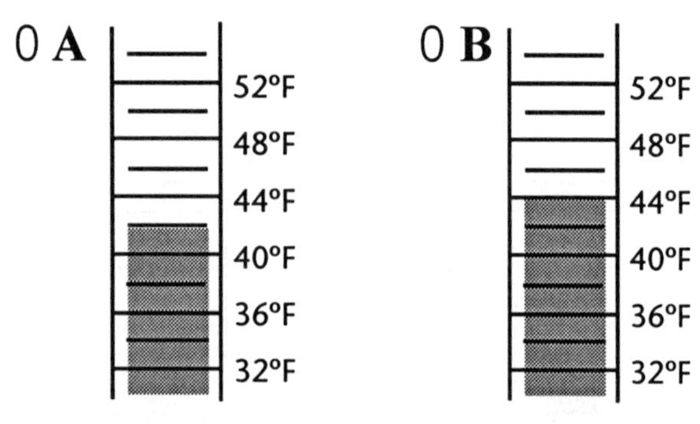

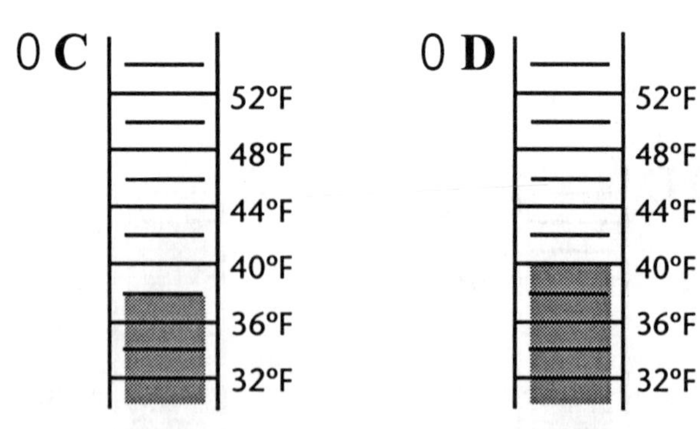

Practice 4.H3

IV.H Use a thermometer to measure temperature

1. What temperature is shown on the thermometer?

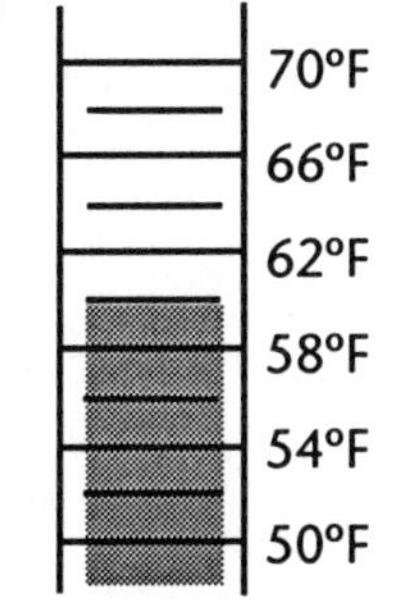

0 **A** 59°F

0 **B** 60°F

0 **C** 61°F

0 **D** 62°F

2. Which thermometer shows 15°C?

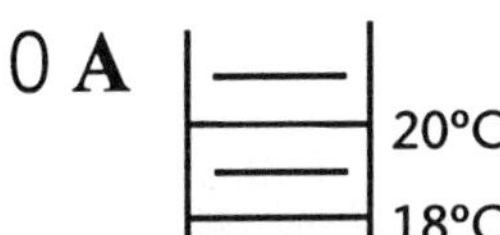

0 **A**

0 **B**

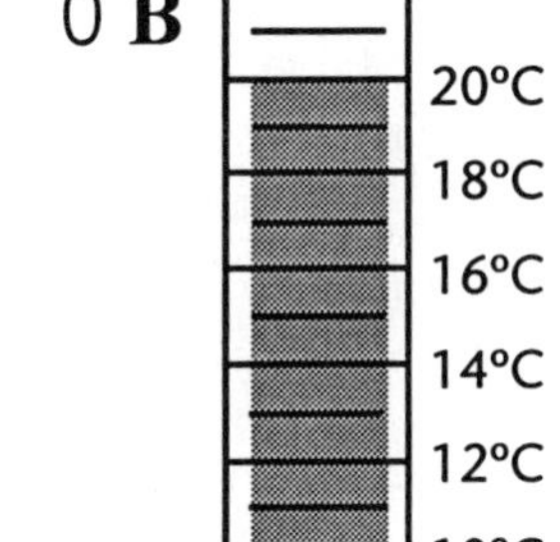

0 **C**

0 **D**

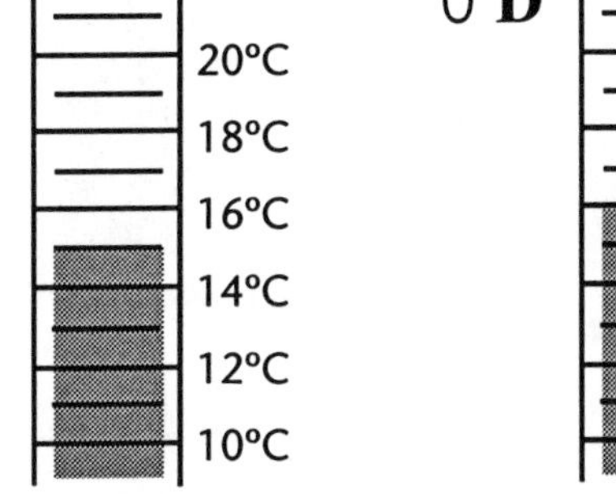

3. What temperature is shown on the thermometer?

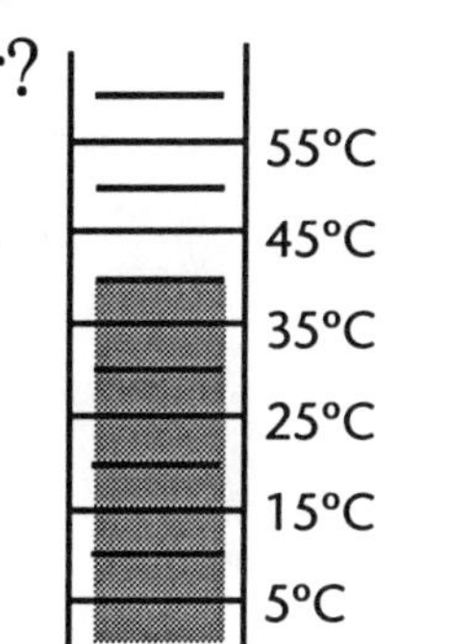

0 **A** 45°C

0 **B** 40°C

0 **C** 39°C

0 **D** 35°C

4. Which thermometer shows 31°F?

0 **A**

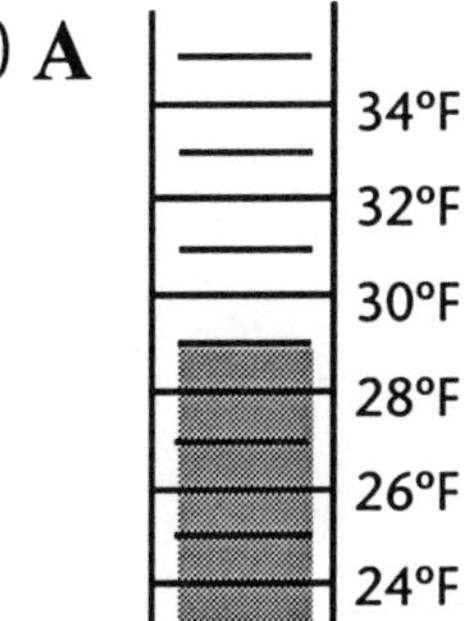

0 **B**

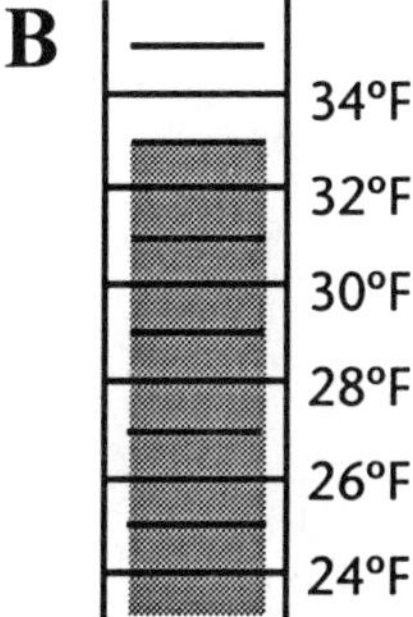

0 **C**

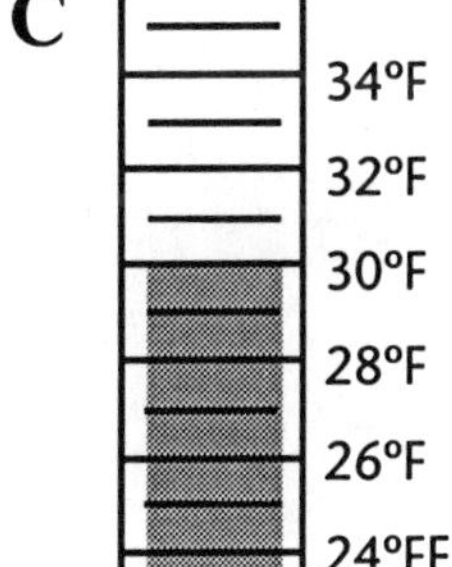

0 **D**

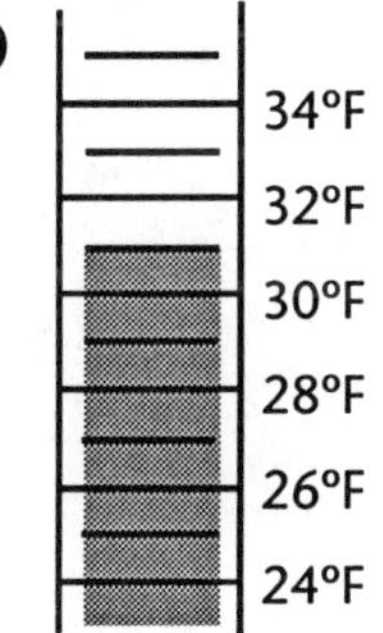

Notes

Probability and Statistics

V. Demonstrate an understanding of probability and statistics

A. Make predictions based on a sampling
B. Interpret information from pictographs, bar graphs, tables, and charts

Notes

Objective 5: Pretest

V.A Make predictions based on a sampling (1-6)

1. Tommy has 5 red marbles, 2 green marbles, 2 blue marbles, and 1 white marble in a bag. He reaches in the bag and takes one marble without looking. What color did he **most** likely take from the bag?

0 **A** white

0 **B** green

0 **C** blue

0 **D** red

2. If you spin the arrow on the spinner, which shape will you **most** likely land on?

0 **A** ✸

0 **B** ❊

0 **C** ✦

0 **D** ☆

3. Mary put the following chips in one bag.

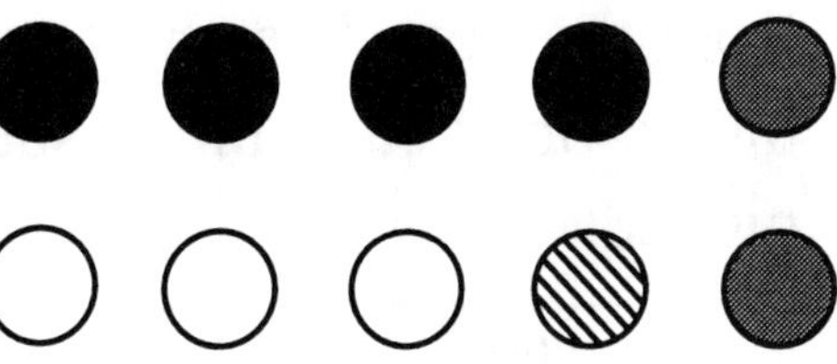

If she reaches into the bag and takes a chip without looking, which kind of chip will she **most** likely pick?

0 **A** ○

0 **B** ●

0 **C**

0 **D**

4. A drawer has 6 blue socks, 3 red socks, 2 yellow socks, and 4 black socks. If you take a sock from the drawer without looking, what color of sock will you **most** likely pick?

0 **A** red

0 **B** yellow

0 **C** black

0 **D** blue

5. Tanya had a box of 100 colored blocks. Without looking, she took 10 blocks from the box. The chart shows the color of each block she picked.

Block	Color
1	Blue
2	Green
3	Green
4	Green
5	Pink
6	Blue
7	Yellow
8	Blue
9	Green
10	Green

Which of these is **most** likely to be true?

0 **A** The box had more green blocks than any other color.

0 **B** There were more yellow blocks than green blocks in the box.

0 **C** There was only 1 pink block in the box.

0 **D** There were only 5 green blocks in the box.

6. Eli has these game pieces in one bag.

If he reaches into the bag and takes one piece without looking, which piece is he **least** likely to pick?

0 **A**

0 **B**

0 **C**

0 **D**

V.B Interpret information from pictographs, bar graphs, tables, and charts (7-12)

The graph shows how many times 5 friends went to Sea World. Use the graph to answer questions 7–8.

Al	✸ ✸ ✸
Tom	✸ ✸
Fran	✸ ✸ ✸ ✸
Kim	✸
Sam	✸ ✸ ✸ ✸ ✸

Each ✸ means 1 trip to Sea World.

7. How many more trips did Fran have than Al?

0 **A** 4

0 **B** 3

0 **C** 2

0 **D** 1

8. Which one shows how to find the number of trips made by Al, Tom, and Sam?

0 **A** 3 + 3 + 4

0 **B** 3 + 1 + 5

0 **C** 3 + 2 + 5

0 **D** 2 + 3 + 1

This graph shows how many books 5 students read during one month.Use the graph to answer questions 9 and 10.

Kate	👓 👓
Edna	👓 👓 👓
Bill	👓 👓 👓 👓
Juan	👓
Sam	👓 👓

Each 👓 means 2 books.

9. How many books did Juan and Sam read in all?

0 **A** 2

0 **B** 6

0 **C** 4

0 **D** 3

10. Which one shows how many more books Edna read than Kate?

0 **A** 3 – 2 = 1

0 **B** 3 + 2 = 5

0 **C** 6 – 4 = 2

0 **D** 6 – 2 = 4

This chart shows how many children were in 3 races. Use the chart to answer questions 11 and 12.

Race	3-legged	Sack	Relay
Number of Students	15	12	6

11. Which graph matches the facts given in the chart?

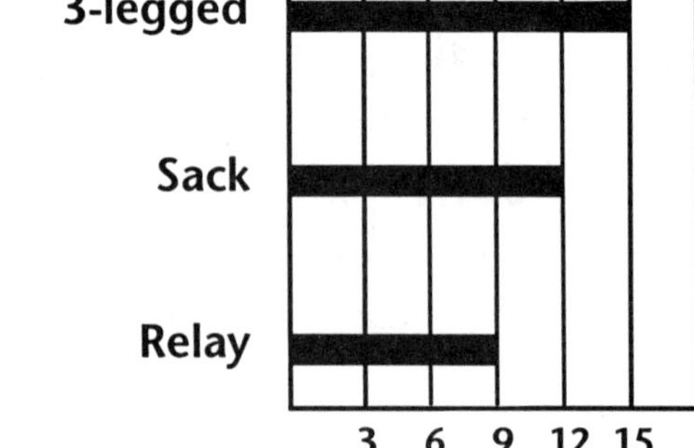

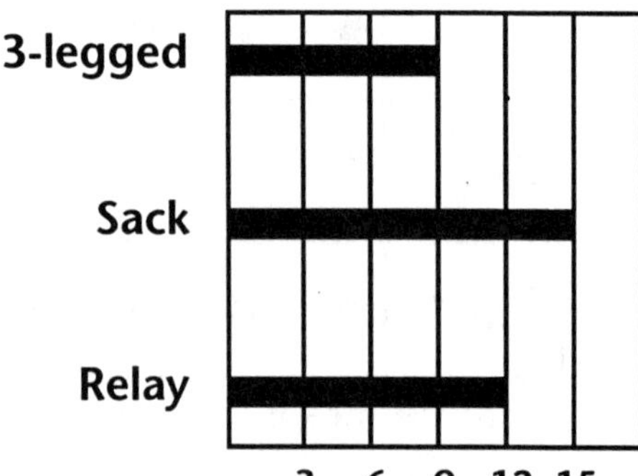

0 B
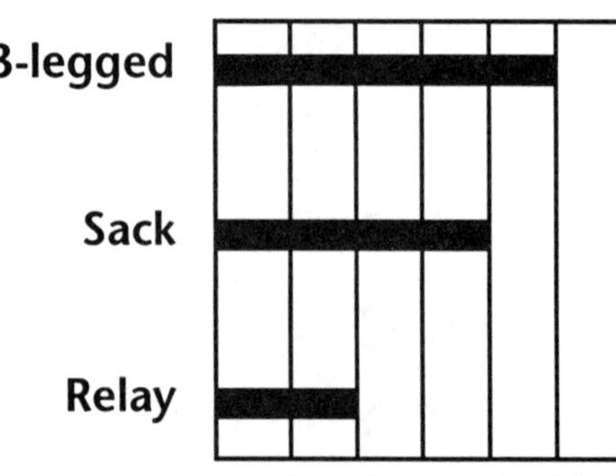

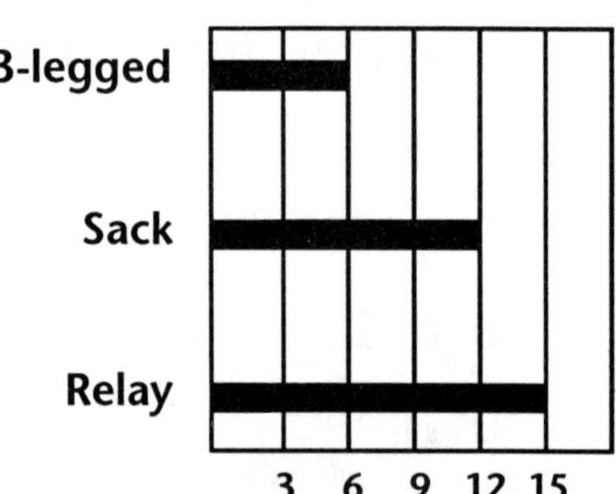

12. Which one shows how many more children were in the sack race than the relay race?

0 **A** 12 + 6 = 18

0 **B** 15 – 12 = 3

0 **C** 12 – 6 = 6

0 **D** 15 – 12 = 3

Practice 5.A1

V.A Make predictions based on a sampling

1. A bag of gum drops has 1 red candy, 3 yellow candies, 2 green candies, and 5 orange candies. If you reach in the bag and take one candy without looking, what color are you **most** likely to get?

0 **A** red

0 **B** green

0 **C** orange

0 **D** yellow

2. If you spin the arrow on the spinner, which letter will you **most** likely land on?

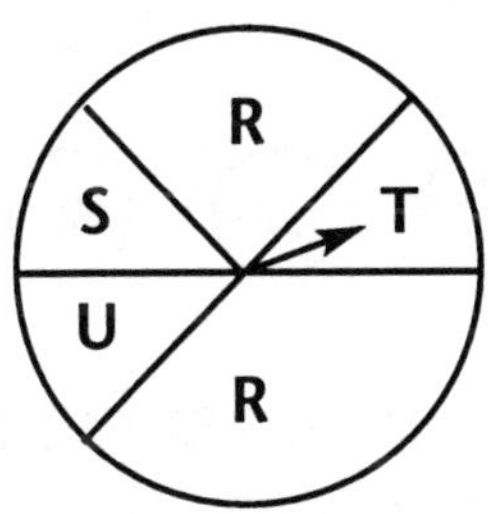

0 **A** S

0 **B** R

0 **C** U

0 **D** T

3. Tina had these game cards.

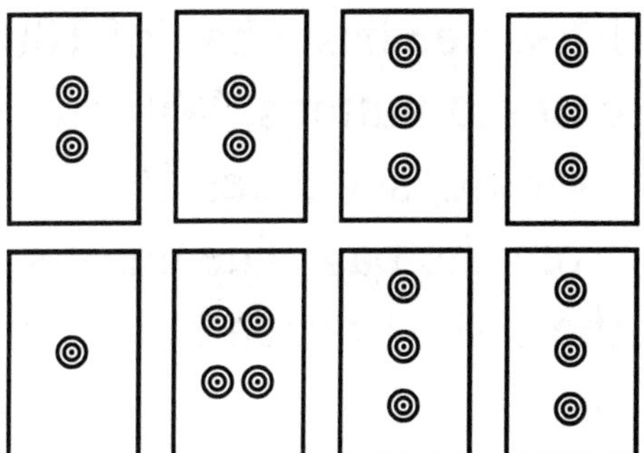

She mixed the cards and put them in a stack. Without looking, she picked a card from the stack. Which card did she **most** likely pick?

0 **A**

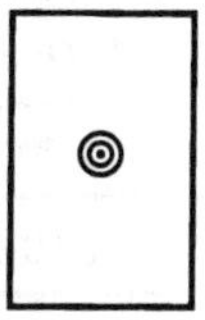

0 **B**

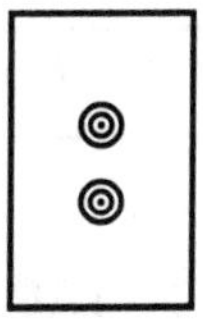

0 **C**

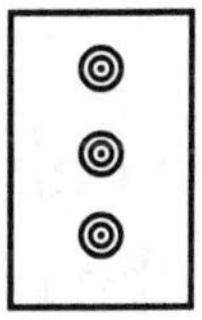

0 **D**

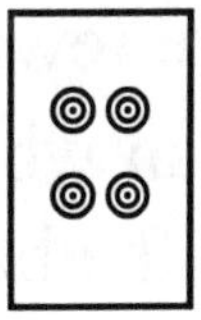

Practice 5.A2

V.A Make predictions based on a sampling

1. Mrs. Lee has a bag of 100 colored buttons. Without looking, she takes 10 buttons from the bag. The chart shows the color of each button she picks.

Button	Color
1	White
2	White
3	Blue
4	Black
5	White
6	Green
7	Black
8	Blue
9	White
10	White

Which of these is most likely to be true?

0 **A** There were only 2 blue buttons in the bag.

0 **B** There were fewer green buttons than white buttons in the bag.

0 **C** There were only 5 white buttons in the bag.

0 **D** There were 50 black buttons in the bag.

2. If you spin the arrow on the spinner, which color are you **most** likely to land on?

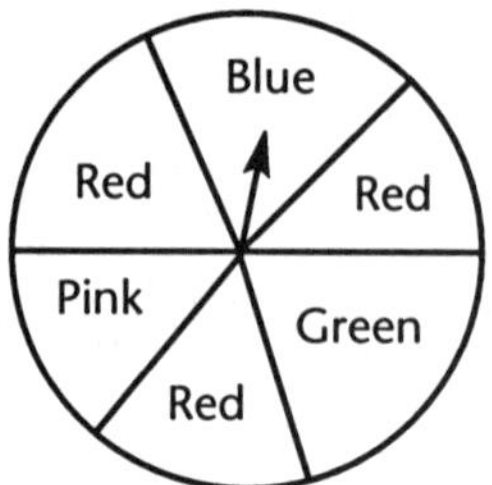

0 **A** Green

0 **B** Blue

0 **C** Pink

0 **D** Red

3. Nancy has these game pieces in her pocket.

If she takes a game piece from her pocket without looking, which piece is she **least** likely to pick?

0 **A** ★

0 **B** ☆

0 **C** 🔔

0 **D** ❄

Practice 5.A3

V.A Make predictions based on a sampling

1. At a carnival, you spin a game wheel like the one below.

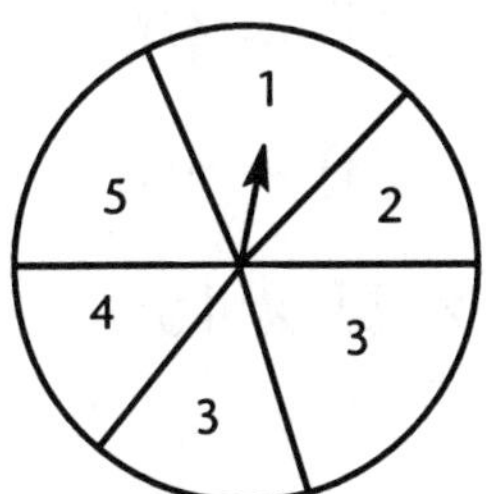

Which number are you **most** likely to land on?

0 **A** 4

0 **B** 3

0 **C** 2

0 **D** 1

2. Bonnie has a cooler of soft drinks. It holds 3 orange sodas, 5 root beers, 4 colas, and 3 lemon-lime sodas. If she takes a drink without looking, what kind of drink is she **most** likely to get?

0 **A** orange

0 **B** cola

0 **C** lemon-lime

0 **D** root beer

3. For a word game, Mrs. Perez put the following slips of paper in a bowl.

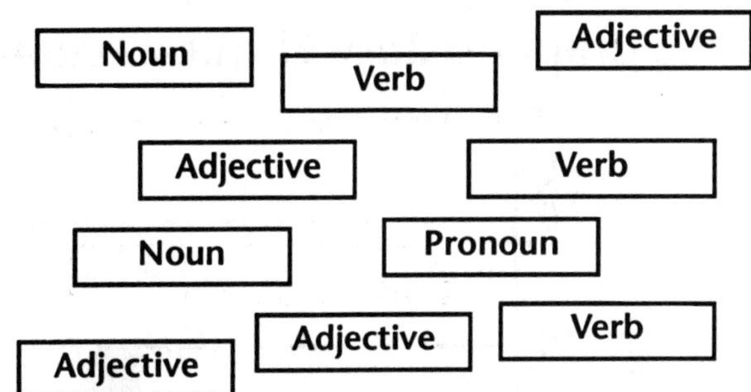

If Ronnie takes a slip of paper from the bowl without looking, which piece is he **least** likely to pick?

0 **A** Verb

0 **B** Adjective

0 **C** Noun

0 **D** Pronoun

Practice 5.B1

V.B Interpret information from pictographs, bar graphs, tables, and charts

The graph shows the number of raffle tickets sold by 3 girls. Use the graph to answer questions 1-4.

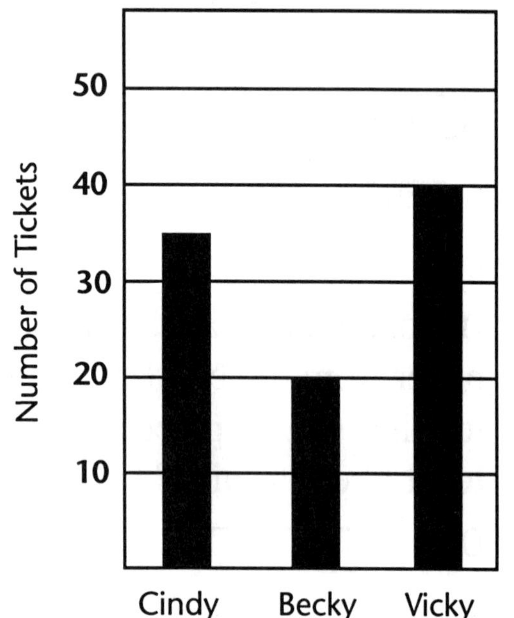

1. Which chart matches the facts in the graph?

0 **A**

Cindy	Becky	Vicky
40	20	50

0 **B**

Cindy	Becky	Vicky
30	20	40

0 **C**

Cindy	Becky	Vicky
35	20	40

0 **D**

Cindy	Becky	Vicky
35	25	45

2. Which one shows how to find the number of tickets sold by all 3 girls?

0 **A** 40 + 20 – 50

0 **B** 35 + 20 + 40

0 **C** 30 + 20 + 50

0 **D** 35 x 25 x 45

3. How many more tickets did Vicky sell than Becky?

0 **A** 60

0 **B** 30

0 **C** 20

0 **D** 15

4. How many tickets did Cindy and Becky sell?

0 **A** 60

0 **B** 55

0 **C** 50

0 **D** 35

Practice 5.B2

V.B Interpret information from pictographs, bar graphs, tables, and charts

The graph shows the number of video games won by 5 children. Use the graph to answer questions 1 and 2.

Celia	☺ ☺ ☺
Larry	☺
Brad	☺ ☺ ☺
Paula	☺ ☺ ☺ ☺ ☺
Juli	☺ ☺ ☺ ☺

Each ☺ means 1 video game won.

1. How many more video games did Paula win than Celia?

0 **A** 8

0 **B** 5

0 **C** 3

0 **D** 2

2. Which is one way to find the number of games won by Larry, Brad, and Juli?

0 **A** 1 + 3 + 4

0 **B** 1 x 3 x 4

0 **C** 1 + 3 – 4

0 **D** 4 + 3 – 1

The graph shows the number of third-grade students who play soccer. Use the graph to answer questions 3 and 4.

Room A	⊙ ⊙ ⊙
Room B	⊙ ⊙ ⊙ ⊙
Room C	⊙ ⊙ ⊙ ⊙ ⊙
Room D	⊙ ⊙
Room E	⊙ ⊙ ⊙ ⊙

Each ⊙ = 2 students.

3. Which room has the **fewest** number of students who play soccer?

0 **A** Room A

0 **B** Room C

0 **C** Room D

0 **D** Room E

4. How many more students in Room C play soccer than in Room A?

0 **A** 16

0 **B** 8

0 **C** 4

0 **D** 2

Practice 5.B3

V.B Interpret information from pictographs, bar graphs, tables, and charts

The chart shows the number of baseball cards owned by 3 students.

Student	Clay	Sue	Tom
Number of Cards	10	5	15

1. Which graph matches the facts in the chart?

0 **A**

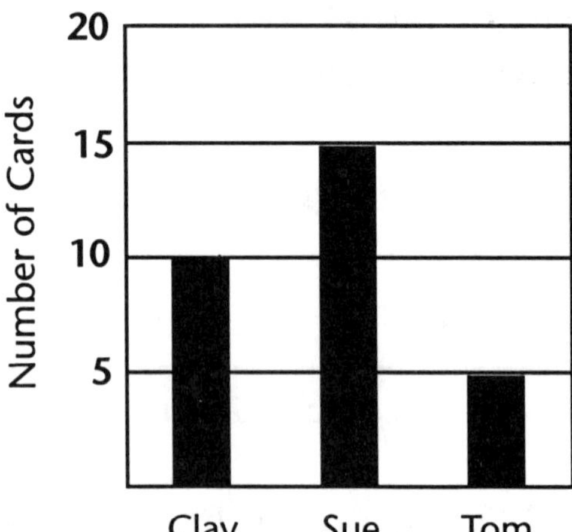

0 **C**

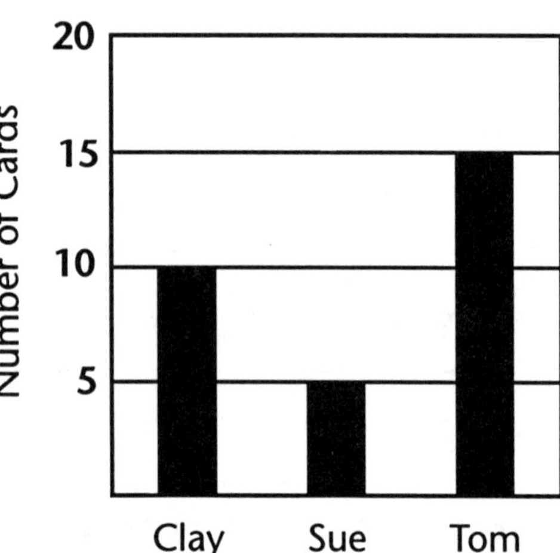

0 **B**

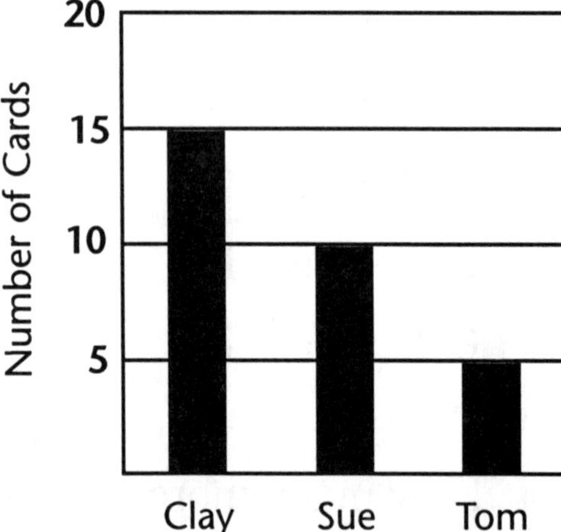

0 **D**

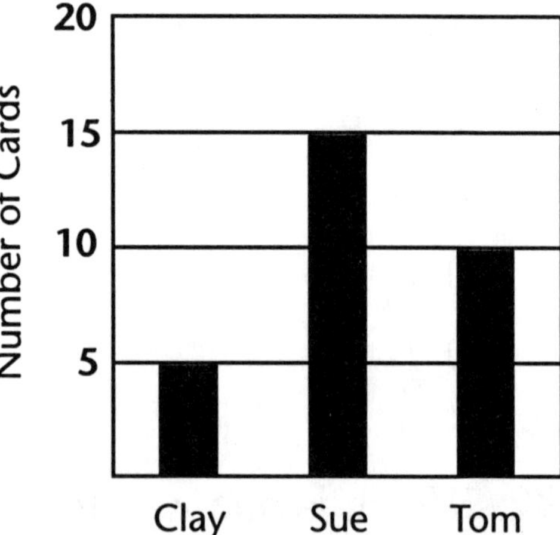

2. Which one shows how many cards the 3 children had in all?

0 **A** 10 + 5 – 15

0 **B** 10 x 5 x 15

0 **C** 10 + 15 – 5

0 **D** 10 + 5 + 15

Appendix

- **Answer Key**
- **Answer Sheets**

Notes

Answer Key: Number Concepts

Objective 1 Pretest (p. 11)

1. B	2. D	3. A	4. D	5. A
6. C	7. C	8. C	9. C	10. D
11. C	12. A	13. B	14. C	15. A
16. C	17. D	18. C	19. C	20. C
21. C	22. D	23. C	24. D	25. C
26. B	27. B	28. B	29. D	30. C
31. B	32. B	33. C	34. C	35. B
36. C	37. B	38. C	39. D	

Practice 1.A1 (p. 18)

1. C 2. D 3. A 4. C 5. D
6. C 7. D

Practice 1.A2 (p. 19)

1. B 2. D 3. A 4. B 5. D
6. D 7. C

Practice 1.A3 (p. 20)

1. C 2. B 3. C 4. C 5. D
6. C 7. B

Practice 1.B1 (p. 21)

1. C 2. D 3. B 4. C 5. A

Practice 1.B2 (p. 22)

1. D 2. C 3. D 4. B 5. A

Practice 1.B3 (p. 23)

1. A 2. A 3. C 4. C 5. B

Practice I.C1 (p. 24)

1. C 2. C 3. A 4. B 5. D
6. C

Practice 1.C2 (p. 25)

1. B 2. B 3. C 4. A 5. D
6. B

Practice 1.C3 (p. 26)

1. C 2. D 3. D 4. D 5. B
6. B

Practice 1.D1 (p. 27)

1. B 2. A 3. A 4. C 5. A

Practice 1.D2 (p. 28)

1. C 2. D 3. B 4. C 5. B

Practice 1.D3 (p. 29)

1. C 2. D 3. B 4. D 5. C

Practice 1.E1 (p. 30)

1. C 2. B 3. B 4. D 5. C

Practice 1.E2 (p. 31)

1. C 2. B 3. C 4. B 5. D

Practice 1.E3 (p. 32)

1. B 2. A 3. C 4. B 5. B

Practice 1.F1 (p. 33)

1. B 2. D 3. C 4. C 5. C
6. C

Practice 1.F2 (p. 34)

1. D 2. B 3. A 4. C 5. C
6. B

Practice 1.F3 (p. 35)

1. A 2. D 3. C 4. D 5. C

Answer Key: Mathematical Relations, Functions, & Algebraic Concepts

Objective 2 Pretest (p. 39)

1. C	2. D	3. C	4. D	5. C
6. D	7. D	8. D	9. B	10. C
11. D	12. D	13. D	14. C	15. A
16. D	17. B	18. D	19. C	20. C
21. B	22. C	23. D	24. B	25. D

Practice 2. A1 (p. 45)

1. C 2. D 3. D 4. C 5. A

Practice 2. A2 (p. 46)

1. C 2. B 3. C 4. D 5. C

Practice 2. A3 (p. 47)

1. B 2. C 3. C 4. B 5. C

Practice 2. B1 (p. 48)

1. D 2. C 3. C 4. A 5. A
6. D

Practice 2. B2 (p. 49)

1. C 2. C 3. D 4. B 5. D
6. A

Practice 2. B3 (p. 50)

1. D 2. D 3. C 4. B 5. C
6. A

Practice 2. C1 (p. 51)

1. B 2. D 3. C 4. B

Practice 2. C2 (p. 52)

1. C 2. D 3. A 4. B

Practice 2. C3 (p. 53)

1. B 2. D 3. C 4. B

Practice 2. D1 (p. 54)

1. C 2. B

Practice 2. D2 (p. 55)

1. B 2. C

Practice 2. D3 (p. 56)

1. C 2. D

Answer Key: Geometric Properties/Relationships

Objective 3 Pretest (p. 59)

1. C	2. D	3. D	4. A	5. C
6. D	7. B	8. C	9. B	10. D
11. D	12. C	13. B	14. D	15. C
16. D	17. B	18. C		

Practice 3. A1 (p. 63)

1. D 2. C 3. B 4. A 5. D
6. B

Practice 3. A2 (p. 64)

1. A 2. D 3. C 4. A 5. D

Practice 3. A3 (p. 65)

1. D 2. B 3. A 4. D 5. C

Practice 3. B1 (p. 66)

1. D 2. A 3. C 4. D

Practice 3. B2 (p. 67)

1. D 2. C 3. C 4. D

Practice 3. B3 (p. 68)

1. D 2. C 3. B 4. C

Practice 3. C1 (p. 69)

1. D 2. B 3. A 4. B

Practice 3. C2 (p. 70)

1. B 2. B 3. D 4. C

Practice 3. C3 (p. 71)

1. D 2. C 3. A 4. D

Practice 3. D1 (p. 72)

1. B 2. C 3. D 4. B

Practice 3. D2 (p. 73)

1. B 2. B 3. C 4. C

Practice 3. D3 (p. 74)

1. C 2. B 3. D 4. C

Answer Key: Measurement Concepts

Objective 4 Pretest (p. 77)

1. C	2. D	3. D	4. C	5. A
6. D	7. B	8. B	9. D	10. B
11. D	12. B	13. C	14. B	15. D
16. B	17. A	18. C	19. D	20. A
21. B	22. D			

Practice 4. A1 (p. 82)

1. B 2. D 3. C 4. C 5. D

Practice 4. A2 (p. 83)

1. A 2. D 3. B 4. B 5. A

Practice 4. A3 (p. 84)

1. D 2. C 3. C 4. A 5. B

Practice 4. B1 (p. 85)

1. C 2. B 3. C 4. C

Practice 4. B2 (p. 86)

1. D 2. B 3. A 4. D

Practice 4. B3 (p. 87)

1. C 2. D 3. D 4. C

Practice 4. C1 (p. 88)

1. C 2. B 3. D 4. B 5. C
6. B

Practice 4. C2 (p. 89)

1. B 2. A 3. C 4. D 5. B
6. C

Practice 4. C3 (p. 90)

1. C 2. B 3. A 4. C 5. D
6. A

Practice 4. D1 (p. 91)

1. C 2. A 3. D 4. C 5. D
6. B

Practice 4. D2 (p. 92)

1. D 2. C 3. D 4. C 5. B
6. C

Practice 4. D3 (p. 93)

1. D 2. C 3. A 4. C 5. B
6. A

Practice 4. E1 (p. 94)

1. C 2. B 3. A 4. D

Practice 4. E2 (p. 95)

1. B 2. C 3. C 4. D

Practice 4. E3 (p. 96)

1. A 2. D 3. B 4. C

Practice 4. F1 (p. 97)

1. C 2. D 3. A 4. B

Practice 4. F2 (p. 98)

1. B 2. C 3. C 4. D

Practice 4. F3 (p. 99)

1. D 2. A 3. C 4. C

Practice 4. G1 (p. 100)

1. B 2. D 3. C 4. B 5. D

Practice 4. G2 (p. 101)

1. B 2. A 3. C 4. C 5. B

Practice 4. G3 (p. 102)

1. D 2. A 3. C 4. C 5. B

Practice 4. H1 (p. 103)

1. C 2. B 3. D 4. A

Practice 4. H2 (p. 104)

1. B 2. D 3. C 4. A

Practice 4. H3 (p. 105)

1. B 2. C 3. B 4. D

Answer Key: Probability and Statistics

Objective 5 Pretest (p. 109)

1. D 2. C 3. B 4. D 5. A
6. C 7. D 8. C 9. B 10. C
11. B 12. C

Practice 5. A1 (p. 113)

1. C 2. B 3. C

Practice 5. A2 (p. 114)

1. B 2. D 3. C

Practice 5. A3 (p. 115)

1. B 2. D 3. D

Practice 5. B1 (p. 116)

1. C 2. B 3. C 4. B

Practice 5. B2 (p. 117)

1. D 2. A 3. C 4. C

Practice 5. B3 (p. 118)

1. C 2. D

Name ______________________________ **Date** ____________

Objective # ________ Pretest

Pretest Answer Sheet

1. Ⓐ Ⓑ Ⓒ Ⓓ	11. Ⓐ Ⓑ Ⓒ Ⓓ	21. Ⓐ Ⓑ Ⓒ Ⓓ	31. Ⓐ Ⓑ Ⓒ Ⓓ
2. Ⓐ Ⓑ Ⓒ Ⓓ	12. Ⓐ Ⓑ Ⓒ Ⓓ	22. Ⓐ Ⓑ Ⓒ Ⓓ	32. Ⓐ Ⓑ Ⓒ Ⓓ
3. Ⓐ Ⓑ Ⓒ Ⓓ	13. Ⓐ Ⓑ Ⓒ Ⓓ	23. Ⓐ Ⓑ Ⓒ Ⓓ	33. Ⓐ Ⓑ Ⓒ Ⓓ
4. Ⓐ Ⓑ Ⓒ Ⓓ	14. Ⓐ Ⓑ Ⓒ Ⓓ	24. Ⓐ Ⓑ Ⓒ Ⓓ	34. Ⓐ Ⓑ Ⓒ Ⓓ
5. Ⓐ Ⓑ Ⓒ Ⓓ	15. Ⓐ Ⓑ Ⓒ Ⓓ	25. Ⓐ Ⓑ Ⓒ Ⓓ	35. Ⓐ Ⓑ Ⓒ Ⓓ
6. Ⓐ Ⓑ Ⓒ Ⓓ	16. Ⓐ Ⓑ Ⓒ Ⓓ	26. Ⓐ Ⓑ Ⓒ Ⓓ	36. Ⓐ Ⓑ Ⓒ Ⓓ
7. Ⓐ Ⓑ Ⓒ Ⓓ	17. Ⓐ Ⓑ Ⓒ Ⓓ	27. Ⓐ Ⓑ Ⓒ Ⓓ	37. Ⓐ Ⓑ Ⓒ Ⓓ
8. Ⓐ Ⓑ Ⓒ Ⓓ	18. Ⓐ Ⓑ Ⓒ Ⓓ	28. Ⓐ Ⓑ Ⓒ Ⓓ	38. Ⓐ Ⓑ Ⓒ Ⓓ
9. Ⓐ Ⓑ Ⓒ Ⓓ	19. Ⓐ Ⓑ Ⓒ Ⓓ	29. Ⓐ Ⓑ Ⓒ Ⓓ	39. Ⓐ Ⓑ Ⓒ Ⓓ
10. Ⓐ Ⓑ Ⓒ Ⓓ	20. Ⓐ Ⓑ Ⓒ Ⓓ	30. Ⓐ Ⓑ Ⓒ Ⓓ	40. Ⓐ Ⓑ Ⓒ Ⓓ

Practice Answer Sheet

Name ______________________________

Date: __________ Practice: # __________	Date: __________ Practice: # __________
1. Ⓐ Ⓑ Ⓒ Ⓓ 2. Ⓐ Ⓑ Ⓒ Ⓓ 3. Ⓐ Ⓑ Ⓒ Ⓓ 4. Ⓐ Ⓑ Ⓒ Ⓓ 5. Ⓐ Ⓑ Ⓒ Ⓓ 6. Ⓐ Ⓑ Ⓒ Ⓓ 7. Ⓐ Ⓑ Ⓒ Ⓓ	1. Ⓐ Ⓑ Ⓒ Ⓓ 2. Ⓐ Ⓑ Ⓒ Ⓓ 3. Ⓐ Ⓑ Ⓒ Ⓓ 4. Ⓐ Ⓑ Ⓒ Ⓓ 5. Ⓐ Ⓑ Ⓒ Ⓓ 6. Ⓐ Ⓑ Ⓒ Ⓓ 7. Ⓐ Ⓑ Ⓒ Ⓓ
Date: __________ Practice: # __________	Date: __________ Practice: # __________
1. Ⓐ Ⓑ Ⓒ Ⓓ 2. Ⓐ Ⓑ Ⓒ Ⓓ 3. Ⓐ Ⓑ Ⓒ Ⓓ 4. Ⓐ Ⓑ Ⓒ Ⓓ 5. Ⓐ Ⓑ Ⓒ Ⓓ 6. Ⓐ Ⓑ Ⓒ Ⓓ 7. Ⓐ Ⓑ Ⓒ Ⓓ	1. Ⓐ Ⓑ Ⓒ Ⓓ 2. Ⓐ Ⓑ Ⓒ Ⓓ 3. Ⓐ Ⓑ Ⓒ Ⓓ 4. Ⓐ Ⓑ Ⓒ Ⓓ 5. Ⓐ Ⓑ Ⓒ Ⓓ 6. Ⓐ Ⓑ Ⓒ Ⓓ 7. Ⓐ Ⓑ Ⓒ Ⓓ

Notes

Notes